Es

Berlin

by

GABRIELLE MACPHEDRAN

and

ADAM HOPKINS

Gabrielle MacPhedran, a journalist and broadcaster,
has written several *Essential* guides
together with Adam Hopkins,
a travel writer and regular contributor
to the *Daily Telegraph*

AA

Produced by AA Publishing

Written by Gabrielle
MacPhedran
and Adam Hopkins
Peace and Quiet section
by Paul Sterry
Original photography by
Adrian Baker

Revised second edition January
1996. First published 1992

Edited, designed and produced by
AA Publishing. © The Automobile
Association 1996.
Maps © The Automobile Association
1996.

Distributed in the United Kingdom
by AA Publishing, Norfolk House,
Priestley Road, Basingstoke,
Hampshire, RG24 9NY.

A CIP catalogue record for this book
is available from the British Library.

ISBN 0 7495 1163 X

The contents of this publication are
believed correct at the time of
printing. Nevertheless, the
publishers cannot be held
responsible for any errors or
omissions or for changes in the
details given in this guide or for the
consequences of any reliance on the
information provided by the same.
Assessments of attractions, hotels,
restaurants and so forth are based
upon the authors' own experience
and, therefore, descriptions given in
this guide necessarily contain an
element of subjective opinion which
may not reflect the publisher's
opinion or dictate a reader's own
experience on another occasion.
**We have tried to ensure accuracy
in this guide, but things do change
and we would be grateful if
readers would advise us of any
inaccuracies they may encounter.**

Published by AA Publishing, a
trading name of Automobile
Association Developments Limited,
whose registered office is Norfolk
House, Priestley Road, Basingstoke,
Hampshire, RG24 9NY.
Registered number 1878835.

Colour separation: L C Repro,
Aldermaston

Printed in Italy by Printers S.R.L.,
Trento

*Front cover picture: Schloss
Charlottenburg*

Contents

Country Distinguishing Signs
On some maps, international distinguishing signs indicate the location of countries around Germany. Thus:

(PL) = Poland

This book employs a simple rating system to help choose which places to visit:

 'top ten'

◆◆◆ do not miss
◆◆ see if you can
◆ worth seeing if you have time

INTRODUCTION

Berlin – one of the world's great cities. Berlin – where disaster and division, symbolised by the Wall that split the city, have yielded to reconciliation. Berlin – once more itself, whole and entire since German reunification in 1990, and now confirmed in its position as the seat of national government and capital of Germany. The visitor cannot ignore the physical and mental marks left by the destruction of World War II and the division of the city, for more than 40 years, into two different and hostile camps. Not surprisingly, as Berlin begins to re-create itself from the ground up, the euphoria following the fall of the Wall has given way to a more sober calculation of the cost of unity to both sides; some tension and suspicion remains. But there is no turning back. And, for all Berliners, the future looks set to be an exciting one.
That is one reason for visiting Berlin. Those who take the historical approach will go further, for this was the city of Hitler's Third Reich, military aggressor turned victim of a war it had itself

An enduring symbol: Brandenburger Tor expressed Prussian Imperialism, Cold War conflict, and finally freedom

provoked. Before that it was the focus of the Weimar Republic, scene of frenzied inflation, intellectual ferment, worker politics and naughty nightclubs. Before that again, it was the capital of an empire with military parades and brisk efficiency on one hand, and a chaotic, teeming, discontented industrial metropolis on the other. Through all this Berlin emerged not just as one of the great capitals of Europe but also one of the cultural capitals of the world. Thanks to a legacy of generous subsidies for the arts in both sides of a divided city, it has world-class museums and theatres, an annual Film Festival of considerable prestige and magnificent classical music-making.

The other main reason for visiting Berlin is the unique atmosphere in the former West. Because of its isolation and the strangeness of its situation, West Berlin developed an informality quite different from that of other German cities. Citizens of the old West were free from conscription, a fact which combined with the general tolerance as an attraction for young people. West Berlin was an 'alternative' city. Mostly, this created a sense of comfort, but there were also pockets of extreme radicalism, as in Kreuzberg, often expressed in disputes over squatting which ended in pitched battles. At the same time, however, it was the prevalence of squatting which helped to preserve many pre-war buildings, calamitously run down during the 1960s and 1970s and in real danger of demolition. These have been done up, often by their former squatters, and are seen as a unique part of the city's heritage and part of a process of gentrification. The baton of alternative radicalism appears to have passed to communities in the old residential parts of Mitte district, in the former East. However, since the decision of the German state government to return to Berlin, these bands of activists, artists, musicians and small entrepreneurs find themselves on prime-value land and increasingly hard pressed by the attentions of property speculators.

Another distinctive element of Berlin has been the presence of 'guest workers', the vast majority of them Turkish, who came during the 1950s and 1960s and settled in the former West

East still meets West in Berlin at Maybachufer's Turkish Market

of the city. Never well assimilated, and still conspicuously poorer than the rest of the population, they lead a separate semi-submerged life, entering the mainstream mainly in the provision of instant food stalls and markets. Unemployment, the cost of German unity, the breakdown of borders within Europe and racial violence have all left their mark on Berlin. Problems exist undoubtedly, but the visitor will find a sense of optimism that is almost tangible.

Berlin Today

Berlin, with just four million people, is an enormous city, covering huge tracts of land. Within its boundaries, both to east and west, lie large lakes and considerable forests. Even in the centre there are large open areas such as the Tiergarten, one-time hunting ground of princes, and the city is pierced by rivers and laced with canals. Great chunks of it, however, are extremely urban; and almost everything is new, due to the destruction of World War II and the building programme following reunification. Amid the newness and rawness, there are some formidable survivals. Kreuzberg, Prenzlauer Berg, and Scheunenviertel retain the shape if not the feel of 19th-century Berlin.

*Bebelplatz, off
Unter den Linden
is a surviving
enclave of the
Hohenzollern city*

Even more important in the look of the city has
been the fragmentary survival, followed by total
reconstruction, of a large sequence of the
principal buildings of Prussian and Imperial
Berlin, running up the great city centre
thoroughfare of Unter den Linden, a name
whose literal meaning is Under the Lime Trees.
It is here that you really feel at the heart of
Berlin. The other place where that used to be
true was at the Berlin Wall, which, mostly
vanished now, wriggled its way until 1989–90
across the centre. The Wall, in German Die
Mauer, was built in 1961 to prevent East
Germans moving to the West, as many
thousands were doing annually. Its demise left a
swathe of dead ground right across the middle
of the city, now under busy construction. The
line taken by the Wall followed the line of
division at the end of the war in 1945. The
historic centre of Berlin was the borough called
Mitte ('Middle'), and that fell entirely on the
eastern side. It includes the grand processional
way of Unter den Linden; Museumsinsel
(Museum Island), with its cathedral and

extraordinary museums; and Alexanderplatz,
one-time meeting point for all Berlin.
West Berlin developed a new focus around the
Kaiser-Wilhelm-Gedächtniskirche. This
imposing neo-Gothic church was destroyed in
World War II and left ruinous as a perpetual
reminder. The open space beside the church,
called the Breitscheidplatz, has become a
haven for hippies, tourists, ice-cream eaters
and dropouts. On the far side of the church, the
Kurfürstendamm, or Ku'damm, runs away in a
westerly direction, with cinemas, restaurants,
brightly lit shops and endlessly flowing crowds.
Most people stay in this area, even today, and
use it as a launching pad in their exploration of
Berlin. Nearby Zoo Station is still probably the
city's best focus of communication, with many
buses converging here, as well as the S-Bahn
and the U-Bahn, Berlin's underground railway
system. These easy transport connections will
also take the visitor out of the city centre into
the surrounding area of lakes and woods, and
southwest to Potsdam, palace-city of
Brandenburg and the Prussian monarch.

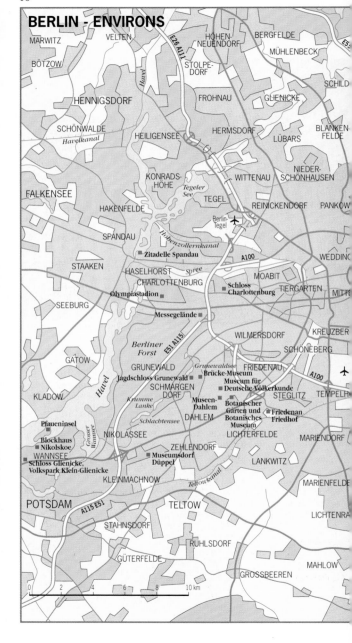

BERLIN - ENVIRONS

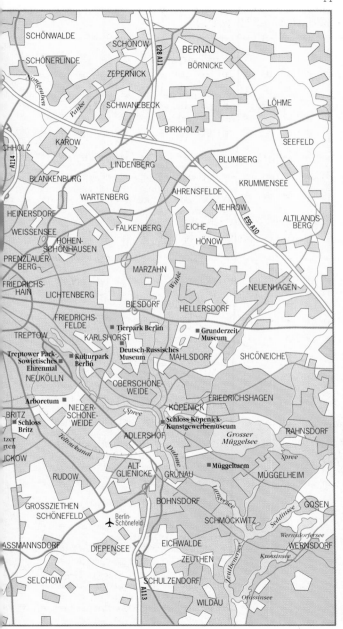

BACKGROUND

Berlin is young in European terms. Little
development took place here till the early
Middle Ages.
Hunters-gatherers passed through in dim
antiquity, leaving little mark among the forests,
lakes and sandy wastes of the country that later
acquired the name of Brandenburg. Scattered
farmers settled in the New Stone Age. The
Romans were delighted to give it a miss,
penetrating only into the south and west of what
later became Germany.
Amidst the wild scenery of Brandenburg –
which today is deeply loved and prized –
settlements slowly developed. Two of these
were on either side of the River Spree,
covering in due course a long, low island in the
middle. The settlements were named Berlin
and Cölln, and the island is the very one
where a royal palace and museums were
later to grow up.
Berlin and Cölln were eastward-looking, river-
trading towns and grew important enough by
the 13th century to receive their own charters.
In 1307, they combined to build a joint town
hall. There were already two churches, and
one, the Marienkirche, hardly damaged in
World War II, still stands. Castles were erected,
to northwest and southeast, on key sites on the
waterways, and later came to act almost as
gateways to the city. Their names were
Spandau and Köpenick, both since replaced
by later buildings – in Spandau a fortress-
citadel, in Köpenick a modest palace.
Otherwise, little survives of the older period,
except for small collections here and there in
museums, of the craft artefacts that were
such a brilliant feature of medieval German
towns and cities.

Beginnings of Greatness
The Germans were a community of the loosest
kind, defined by a language and in due course
the Christian religion (in which a good deal of
forest magic still remained). As the Roman
Empire faded, the Frankish empire of
Charlemagne and his descendants rose to
take its place. Little by little, this transmuted

Marienkirche is a monument to the faith and wealth of the medieval city

itself into a German Empire stretching right across central Europe. It was elective, not hereditary and went by the name of the Holy Roman Empire of the German Nation. Brandenburg was part of it, a 'Mark' or border territory. In 1356 it was decided that seven German rulers should act as the chief electors of the German emperor. One of these was to be the ruler of the Mark of Brandenburg, known henceforward as the Elector of Brandenburg.

Berlin and Cölln, meanwhile, had joined the Hanseatic League of trading cities and showed a remarkable sense of independence. It took many a contest between the Hohenzollern family – from whom the Electors of Brandenburg were drawn – before the towns' independence was finally suppressed.

BACKGROUND

It was not until the 17th century, during the long reign of the Great Elector, Friedrich Wilhelm I (1620–88), that Brandenburg began to surface as a real power. Growing, industrious Berlin and a princely Postdam a short way southwest became a kind of dual focus. Under Friedrich Wilhelm and particularly his son Friedrich III, stately baroque buildings were erected. In Potsdam, from 1660, a great Stadtschloss or Town Palace began to go up. In Berlin, as well as a palace on the island, a magnificent Arsenal was constructed on Unter den Linden, with contributions from Andreas Schlüter, first of a chain of outstanding Berlin architects and sculptors. A little way out of the city, though now in the city centre, the pretty palace of Charlottenburg went up for Sophie Charlotte, wife of Friedrich III.

Another big change in the period was the arrival of thousands of Huguenot craftsmen, persecuted in France but welcomed by Friedrich Wilhelm. Fragments of French still survive in Berlin dialect, and the Huguenots' cemetery (the Alte Französiche Friedhof) is an interesting place to visit. It lies along an improbable-looking lane through a housing estate, by the tram terminus on the corner of Pflugstrasse and Wöhlerstrasse.

To Prussia with luggage: many French émigrés found work in the city

Prussian Berlin

Friedrich III crowned himself King of Prussia in
1701, and became Friedrich I of the new state.
This was a critical moment, making Prussia the
power base of the German-speaking peoples,
with Berlin as their focus, rather than Vienna
(main city of the old Holy Roman Empire).
Friedrich I's son, Friedrich Wilhelm I of Prussia,
the so-called Soldier-King (1688–1740), carried
the process further, organising a bureaucracy –
one of the chief features of Prussia's later
dominance – and building up an army. This was
somewhat weakened by his predilection for
giants, sought out all over Europe as his
guardsmen and sometimes sent to him as
human gifts by other rulers. The Soldier-King
was odd in other ways as well. He had a savage
temper, not far short of madness, and carried a
swagger stick with which he would attack those
who irritated him, cracking teeth and breaking
noses. He made ferocious efforts to repress his
son, later Friedrich II (1712–1786, king from
1740), known as Frederick the Great.
Young Friedrich, as crown prince, tried to
escape from his father and was imprisoned for
military desertion. His closest friend, most
probably his lover, was executed before his
eyes. Succeeding to the throne, however,
Friedrich carried on his father's tradition of

efficiency and militarism, using Unter den Linden, and much of the remainder of the city centre, as a kind of glorified parade ground. Simultaneously, he plunged Prussia into the vortex of the European power struggle, and provoked the rest of Europe into challenging him in the bitter Seven Years War (1756–63). During this, Berlin was briefly occupied. By the time he died Friedrich had made Prussia the leading state of continental Europe. On Unter den Linden, he built the Berlin Opera House (all attendance was by royal invitation). In Potsdam, he created the brilliant small-scale palace of Sanssouci and lived there, in all-male company, speaking in French and passing his time with luminaries such as Voltaire.

After his death, the declining strength of Prussia was no match for the might of Napoleon. Following a humiliating defeat at Jena, Berliners had to watch Napoleon come riding in triumph into the Prussian capital, under the Brandenburg Gate.

The French era was brief and made little impression. But after the Prussian restoration in 1815 it was clear that reform was now in order in Berlin. Army and bureaucracy were tightened up and strengthened. The two Humboldt brothers, both trained in the Prussian civil service, emerged to become symbolic founding fathers of a great Berlin academic tradition. Alexander (1769–1859) was the greatest naturalist and explorer of his day; Wilhelm (1767–1835) created the Humboldt University, which shone like a beacon in Berlin until the time of Hitler. The philosopher Hegel taught there; so did Albert Einstein.

It is no accident at all that Berlin has continuously produced a stunning range of intellectual achievement, right across the sciences and the arts, including architecture. The neo-classical buildings of Karl Friedrich Schinkel (1781–1841), also a romantic painter, contribute especially to the city's special character today. There is a Schinkel Museum just off Unter den Linden at the Museumsinsel end. Berlin has also been a great generator of style, starting in the 1830s with the evolution of that comfortable type of furniture and décor known as Biedermeier.

Humboldt University, where students have studied Hegel's dialectics and Einstein's theory of relativity

The dominant figure of late 19th-century Prussia was Count Otto von Bismarck, a member of Prussia's Junker aristocracy who became a civil servant and eventually Prime Minister in Berlin. Under his guidance, Prussia smashed the armies of Austria in 1866, and was thus able to unite the northern German people into a nation-state for the first time, in 1871.

Heavy industries began making their mark on Berlin from the middle of the 19th century. The great Borsig plant, which made rails and locomotives, features in many contemporary paintings and is now a national monument. By the end of the century, electricity had arrived, and it was above all the demand for

BACKGROUND

electrical goods which fuelled the industries of Berlin. Siemens, for example, had its origins at about this time.

Hundreds of thousands of the rural poor flocked in from Brandenburg and further east to work in the new industries. The newcomers were housed in huge tenements, consisting of courtyard behind courtyard, often grand on the exterior but progressively dreary in their deeper recesses and sometimes with the factory in the same complex. An intensely lived slum life grew up in the Berlin tenements and alleys, with its own distinctive dialect.

Workers, increasingly unionised, called for greater political and economic freedom, but met nothing but repression. Here were to be found the roots of German socialism and it was here, among the labouring masses of Berlin and the German cities, that Karl Marx believed the Revolution would begin. Berlin boroughs such as Wedding and Moabit were the centre for this vigorous, dissident, proletarian life.

The iron fist emerged from the velvet glove when cavalry attacked rioters in 1892

This was also the time of Jugendstil – the German version of Art Nouveau – and the best city blocks mix solid grandeur with its decorative playfulness. Meanwhile, the intellectual life of the city carried on unabated.

The Weimar Years

World War I came as a catastrophe for
Germany. Berlin itself was never enthusiastic,
except in the first heady days of hostilities.
Popular demands for peace were matched by
demands for social justice, for a new
constitution, freedom, equality and socialism.
Kaiser Wilhelm II delayed, then abdicated in
1918. A new Republic was proclaimed from the
balcony of the Reichstag and a government of
the Social Democratic Party was formed. At the
same time, the revolutionary leader, Karl
Liebknecht, proclaimed a rival, revolutionary
Republic from the balcony of the royal palace.
The official government brought in elite bands
of the army and specially formed right-wing
units called the Freikorps, funded by
industrialists. Whole areas of Berlin were in the
grip of revolution, demanding a Communist
system of organisation. Karl Liebknecht and his
fellow-leader Rosa Luxemburg were captured
by the Freikorps and shot. Rosa Luxemburg's
body was dumped in the Landwehr Canal. A
plaque now marks the spot. In the end, the
revolution failed. Berlin nevertheless remained
a hotbed of radical sentiment.

The new system of government, under constant
attack from both the left and right, acquired the
name of the Weimar Republic. In Berlin, an
attempted right-wing coup – the Kapp putsch –
was defeated by a left-wing general strike. In
1923 a right-wing politician named Adolf Hitler
also failed in an attempted coup – in Munich –
and was briefly imprisoned. Worker restlessness
meanwhile terrified the ruling classes.
Throughout these years, Germany staggered
under the humiliation both of a crushing defeat
and an impossible burden of war reparations.
Soon the country experienced the world's first
episode of hyperinflation, with barrow loads of
notes required to buy a cabbage. Some relief,
though, was on the way. Fearful of Communist
revolution, the Americans now made an effort to
aid economic recovery through the so-called
Dawes Plan. Even so, the situation was dire,
with millions out of work and no such thing as
unemployment benefit. Many of the people in
Berlin as elsewhere were close to starving.
Paradoxically, 1920s Berlin was also a time and

BACKGROUND

Theatre director Max Reinhardt (1873–1943), part of the 'Weimar Culture' renaissance of art and creativity

a place unrivalled for freedom and creativity. What came to be known as the 'Weimar Culture' was marked by a level of high achievement in virtually every field, whether scientific or artistic. A tiny sample of Berlin's high achievers would produce names like Thomas and Heinrich Mann, Rainer Maria Rilke and Erich Kästner in literature; Bertolt Brecht and Erwin Piscator, Kurt Weill and Max Reinhardt in theatre; George Grosz, John Heartfield and Käthe Kollwitz as artists committed to political comment and satire; Arnold Schönberg, Otto Klemperer and Wilhelm Furtwängler in music; Fritz Lang, Joseph von Sternberg and Marlene Dietrich in film; in architecture Walter Gropius and Mies van der Rohe. Jazz (later to be outlawed by the Nazis as decadent) was played everywhere. Nightclubs, cabarets and cinemas sprang up all over the city, particularly in the Ku'damm area. Gender was bent, conventions shattered. The black American Josephine Baker, one of many such entertainers, stripped naked on stage every night. Nothing was impossible and nothing was forbidden – or so it seems now. Hitler's Nazi party was advancing strongly throughout the country, though much less so in Berlin. In 1926, Joseph Goebbels was appointed to win over the city. He built up a party structure and conducted marches and rallies of the 'Brownshirts'– Stormtroopers – in predominantly working class and left wing areas of the city like Wedding. The riposte was

Treading the boards: the austere décor of Brecht's house echoes his style

fierce, and pitched battles in the Berlin streets became a daily event – but the nightmarish message of the National Socialists began to appear to many like a gleam of hope.

It was the desperation of the times that caused the Weimar government to try to use the Nazis to suppress the Bolsheviks.

Following an increase in the vote for Hitler in 1930, they little by little brought the Nazis into the government. An arson attack on the Reichstag, on 28 February 1933, was Hitler's pretext to seize control. Henceforth he made his position unassailable, and became dictator of Germany.

Hitler and World War II

The first concentration camp was set up in Dachau in 1933. It received trade unionists and Jews, and anybody else whose ideology differed from that propounded by the National Socialists. This included church leaders opposed to fascism (not all were), political dissidents, homosexuals and any 'criminal element'. The writing was on the wall and the slow exodus of left wing and Jewish artists, scientists, writers and musicians from Berlin became a flood. The loss of these, and of the others who remained and were subsequently killed, impoverished the city immeasurably.

In May 1933 came the Buchverbrennung – a public burning of huge piles of books conflicting with Nazi ideology, opposite Berlin's university.

Anti-Semitic attacks became so vicious and yet so frequent over several years that when, on the night of 9 November 1938, rampaging crowds of Stormtroopers in civilian clothes smashed up the majority of the city's 29 synagogues, destroyed shops and homes and attacked Jews in the street, most Berliners merely averted their eyes. This was called 'Kristallnacht' because of the sight and sound of breaking glass.

There was opposition in Berlin, but not enough to halt the Nazis' ambitions. War was next on the agenda. Hitler proceeded with the brutal enlargement of the German state until, at last, in 1939, following his annexation of Poland, Britain and France declared war. Hitler believed the contest would be brief. At first, he seemed to be right. German troops swept through France and pushed the British off continental Europe. But in due course, the Soviet Union too was drawn into the war and then the United States. From then on, little by little, despite the impossible sacrifices he demanded from his people, Hitler's fate was sealed.

Berlin meanwhile was torn to pieces by massive Allied bombing raids. Destruction was completed during the final days of the war, in which the Fall of Berlin was the key event. Soviet troops completely encircled the city, but it was only when the fighting reached the

Teufelsberg, the Devil's Mountain, created entirely out of war rubble

Reichstag that Hitler acknowledged defeat. He married his mistress, Eva Braun, and committed suicide.

Little was left of Berlin except for gaunt and burnt out buildings and millions of tons of rubble. Uncountable lives were lost among the Russians, the German army and the civilian population. The surviving women of Berlin - there being few men left - became known as the 'Trümmerfrauen' or 'rubble women', as they cleared enough debris to build a mountain in the west of the city.

Berlin Divided: Airlift and Wall

As previously arranged among the Allied leaders, administration of the city was divided between the Soviets, British, French and Americans. German forces surrendered on 8 May 1945 but the British, French and American forces did not take over the administration of their sectors from the Soviets until they arrived in the city in the early days of

July. When they did, they found themselves encircled by a sea of Soviet soldiery and Soviet political control.

Free elections in the Eastern sector were quickly set aside. Nominal control was in the hands of former German Communists who had spent the war years in the Soviet Union. On the Western side, the order given by the Allies was for the gradual re-establishment of a democratic structure. As the two systems grew up in a divided nation, Germany became a theatre of conflict between the Communists and the 'Free World', with Berlin as a microcosm of the whole.

Differing ideologies made co-operation impossible, and the Soviets wanted the Allies out of West Berlin. The crunch came in June 1948 over the introduction of the Deutschmark in the Western zone and the Soviet rejection of

West Berlin's air-lift lifeline is commemorated in a memorial at Tempelhof airport

it in favour of their own system.

The Berliners' vote went to the new Deutschmark. That night, the Soviets began the blockade of Berlin by switching off electricity supplies and cutting road and rail communications. The overall commander in West Berlin was General Lucius Clay. Under his inspired leadership the Allies responded by attempting to supply the whole of their sector of the city by air. At first it seemed that the city would starve, but within weeks, new runways were being built at Tempelhof and Gatow airports and a new airport was constructed at Tegel. Aircraft, loaded with supplies, were landing every 30 seconds. On 12 May 1949, the Soviet leader, Joseph Stalin, finally called off the blockade, thus tacitly admitting the Allies were in Berlin to stay. West Berliners, heavily subsidised by the Allies as a showcase for their economic system, now slowly began to prosper. The city even managed to retain its position as Germany's main industrial centre. East Berlin became the capital of a newly established German Democratic Republic (DDR).

Here matters soon went from bad to worse economically. On 16 June 1953, hearing their workloads were to be increased, construction workers marched on government headquarters. After 24 hours of a confused popular rising, the Soviets brought out the tanks. Deaths and executions followed. Order was restored in East Berlin but it remained highly repressive. Inflamed by the prohibition of free movement and travel, lured by the material glitter of the West, great numbers of East Germans annually used West Berlin as their gateway to a new life in the West.

The response was the construction of the so-called Anti-Fascist Wall. In summer 1961 the whole of West Berlin was walled in and the citizens of the East walled out. On the western side, the wall gradually acquired graffiti and public viewing points. On the eastern side however, the Wall was backed by a no man's land, surveyed from sentry towers by armed soldiers. Many people died trying to cross to the West.

BACKGROUND

Rauthaus Schöneberg became the seat of West Berlin's government after the Blockade

Thus began one of the strangest periods in the life of the city. Under the complicated regulations for control, soldiers of four foreign armies were seen on the streets. Soviet troops came into West Berlin to change the guard at their War Memorial on Strasse des 17 Juni and took their turn in guarding Rudolf Hess, Hitler's one-time deputy and the solitary prisoner held in Spandau gaol, deep in the British sector. Spying was rife, providing material for such popular writers as John le Carré and Len Deighton.

John F Kennedy came to Berlin in 1963 as the young American President on whose shoulders the hopes of a genuinely free world appeared to ride. His phrase 'Ich bin ein Berliner' rang across the city and world, to show that America would not surrender this symbolic Western bastion, however exposed it was. This was also a period when young West

Berliners began to question the ideological system under which they lived. Their protests were put down with a violence that shocked observers. In West Germany this period saw the emergence of the Red Army/Bader Meinhof terrorist faction, striking against what it saw as capitalist excess.

Meanwhile West Berlin continued to develop in its own idiosyncratic way, attracting the 'alternative' young from other states. Heavy subsidy helped the arts to flourish in both halves of the city. West Berlin acquired an avant-garde reputation. East Berlin may have seemed a little old fashioned by comparison, but theatre, opera and music flourished here as in the West.

The City United

The Wall was breached on 9 November 1989. Events had been pointing that way for some while but when it happened, it was still almost unbelievable. Nothing appeared more symbolic of a new order in Europe than crowds toasting each other in champagne by the Brandenburg Gate and surging over and through the Wall.

Earlier in 1989, some Eastern bloc states underwent anti-Soviet and generally anti-Communist revolutions and in the autumn, Hungary opened its borders to the west. In Berlin it was an almost chance remark by a party official at a press conference which implied that citizens of East Berlin would not be stopped if they tried to enter the West. Guards at the border crossings had no warning. When joyous crowds swept down on them, they stood aside and let the people pass. It was not long before the Wall itself was being demolished.

In a period of euphoria and almost incredible optimism, Chancellor Helmut Kohl, leader of West Germany, saw that a weakened USSR had neither the will nor the wish to respond and swept on towards German reunification. Some say he carried the people with him, others that he railroaded them into unification. By 1990, Germany was one again.

Berlin entered the 1990s as the capital of reunited Germany and became the seat of

BACKGROUND

government once again in June 1991, after much debate. Sad to say, the optimism of 1990 ebbed rapidly. The first and perhaps the gravest problem was unemployment sweeping former East Germany, not excluding East Berlin. Businesses which had previously produced only to government order encountered a cut-throat competition for which they were entirely unprepared.

For the tourist, there will inevitably be changes over and above the new accessibility of the whole city. The division of the city has meant that everything – from football grounds to

Looking over the city from Rathaus Schöneberg

museums – has been duplicated. With the reduction of subsidies there will undoubtedly be amalgamations of museums, closures of theatres and rearrangements on a grand scale in the long term. In the light of this, it is likely that this book, as up-to-date as possible at the time of publication, may not always have the latest details.

Over and above its problems, Berlin remains an electric, even a magnetic city, and, as always, a crucible of history. Not to see it would be to miss what may well be Europe's most fascinating capital.

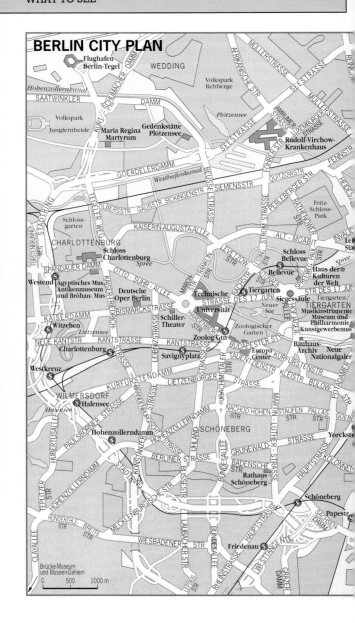

BERLIN CITY PLAN

Flughafen
Berlin-Tegel

WEDDING

Hohenzollernkanal
SAATWINKLER

DAMM

Volkspark
Rehberge

Plötzensee

Volkspark
Jungfernheide

Maria Regina
Martyrum

Gedenkstätte
Plötzensee

Rudolf-Virchow-
Krankenhaus

GOERDELERDAMM

Westhafenkanal

SIEMENSSTR

Fritz-
Schloss-
Park

Schloss-
garten

CHARLOTTENBURG

Schloss
Charlottenburg

Spree

KAISERIN-AUGUSTA-ALLEE

ALT - MOABIT

Schloss
Bellevue

Bellevue

Westend

Ägyptisches Mus
Antikenmuseum
und Bröhan- Mus

SPANDAUER DAMM

OTTO - SUHR - ALLEE

Deutsche
Oper Berlin

Technische
Universität

STRASSE DES 17 JUN

Tiergarten

Siegessäule

Haus der
Kulturen
der Welt

STR DES 17 JU

TIERGARTEN
Musikinstrumente
Museum und
Philharmonie
Kunstgewerbemus

KAISERDAMM

Witzleben

Lietzensee

BISMARCKSTRASSE

Schiller-
Theater

Neuer
See

NEUE KANTSTR

KANTSTRASSE

Zoolog Gtn

Zoologischer
Garten

Bauhaus-
Archiv

Neue
Nationalgaler

Charlottenburg

KANTSTRASSE

Savignyplatz

Europa
Center

KURFÜRSTENSTR

Westkreuz

KURFÜRSTENDAMM

LIETZENBURGER STR

KLEIST- STR

BÜLOW-

WILMERSDORF

Halensee

NACHOD HOHEN-
STR

STAUFEN-
STR

PALLAS-
STR

Hohenzollerndamm

SCHÖNEBERG

Yorckstr

BERLINER STRASSE

GRUNEWALD- STRASSE

BADENSCHE
STR

Rathaus
Schöneberg

Schöneberg

Papestr

HUNDEKEHLE- STR

WIESBADENER STR

Friedenau

Brücke-Museum
und Museen-Dahlem
0   500   1000 m

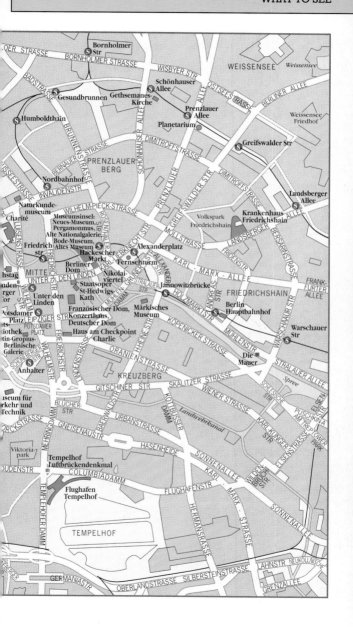

WHAT TO SEE

◆◆◆
ÄGYPTISCHES MUSEUM
Schlossstrasse 70, Map p 30–1
The Egyptian Museum houses only part of an outstanding collection begun in 1698 by the Elector Friedrich III. The rest now forms the splendid collection in the **Bode-Museum** in the East. The star exhibit in Charlottenburg is the head of Queen Nefertiti, sneaked out of the future Soviet sector of East Berlin in the final days of World War II.

There are other works of sculpture here, along with bronzes, papyrus, jewellery, mummy masks, vases and musical instruments from 5000 BC to AD 300.

Also on display is the 2,000-year-old Kalabasha Mounumental Gate, presented by the Egyptian Government in recognition of German help in preserving archaeological monuments during the building of the Aswan High Dam.
Open: Tuesday to Friday 09.00–17.00hrs; Saturday and Sunday 10.00–17.00hrs.

◆◆
ALEXANDERPLATZ
Map p 44–5
Known as 'Alex', the Alexanderplatz was the focal point of old Berlin before the war and served as the centre for East Berlin during the years of Soviet domination.

Famous as a meeting place, it has played a part in almost all popular revolutions, up to and including November 1989. Alexanderplatz forms a hub at the top of the grand processional way leading up via Unter den Linden from the Brandenburg Gate. Once it was a comfortable, crowded, seedy kind of place (best described in Alfred Döblin's 1920s novel of metropolitan low life, *Berlin Alexanderplatz*, later filmed by Fassbinder).

As the showpiece of Communist East Berlin, it was transformed into a huge, open space, ringed by massive Socialist architecture and bordered to the east by a 12-lane highway. Today, as the showpiece of a united capital city, there are plans afoot to transform it once more. The Brunnen der Völkerfreundenschaft (Friendship of the People's Fountain), the World Clock (which tells you the time in such places as Ulan-Bator and Novosibirsk), and the Fernsehturm (the tall television tower erected as an act of grandiloquent pride in defiance of the West) look set to remain in place, albeit spruced up. New plans include the building of sophisticated tower blocks and all the essentials of a modern downtown centre.

Certainly as the months pass, Alexanderplatz becomes a more and more convivial public space. Nearby are the **Rotes Rathaus** and the **Nikolaiviertel** and across Spandauer Strasse is the lovely green space of Marx-Engels Forum, where the two old gentlemen still preside (for who knows how much longer?) over the bronze reliefs of triumphant workers.

◆◆◆
ALTE NATIONALGALERIE
Museumsinsel, Map p 44–5
The setting is one of the great mock-classical buildings of Museumsinsel, in this case a vast, pollution-blackened Corinthian temple of 1866-76, built originally for state receptions. Modern visitors duck in by a door below. Inside, the entrance hall has fine sculptures by Gottfried Schadow, but the bulk of the exhibits are 19th-century European paintings. Some of the most interesting are the ones concerned with Berlin. Look out in particular for Menzel's charming studies of Frederick the Great at Potsdam, and the paintings of military parades

The Rotunda in the Altes Museum

on Unter den Linden by Franz
Krüger (1797-1857). These are
countered by a huge Menzel
scene of the interior of a Berlin
steelworks. Note also Walter
Leistikow's romantically
gloomy view of the
Grunewaldsee (1895). French
Impressionists are well
represented here.
Open: Tuesday to Sunday
09.00–17.00hrs.

ALTES MUSEUM
Marx-Engels-Platz, Map p 44–5
The Old Museum is more than
just that – it is Berlin's oldest,
built by Karl Freidrich Schenker
and considered one of his finest
works. Until the final decision is
made on the nature of its
permanent collection, the
museum is home to temporary
exhibitions only. It is worth
popping in anyway, to see the
magnificent rotunda just inside
the entrance.
Open: Tuesday to Sunday
09.00–17.00hrs.

ANTIKENMUSEUM
Schlossstrasse 1, Map p 30–1
The museum of Greek and
Roman antiquities is housed in a
former barracks immediately
opposite the Ägyptisches
Museum in Charlottenburg, and
is part of the fabulous collection
of antiquities dispersed after
World War II. The rest is now in
the **Pergamon Museum** on
Museumsinsel (see page 61). In
the Antiken Museum, you will
find Minoan, Mycenaean,
Etruscan, Greek and Roman
artefacts – vases, bronzes and
glassware. The star exhibits

are silverwork and jewellery
from 2000BC exhibited in the
basement Schatzkammer
(Treasury). The treasure of
Roman silver found at
Hildesheim in northwestern
Germany is also on display.
Open: Monday to Thursday
09.00–17.00hrs; Saturday and
Sunday 10.00–17.00hrs.

◆

BAUHAUS-ARCHIV
Klingelhöferstrasse 13,
Map p 36–7
The 'Archiv' is in fact a museum
and library on the edge of
Tiergarten. Though short-lived,
the Bauhaus has been hugely
influential in the art and
architecture of the 20th century
– partly through stark and
often box-like buildings, but also
in brilliant paintings,
incomparable typography, and
furniture designs still in
production today.
The Bauhaus was a highly
original art school, where artists
and craftsmen worked together
in a common cause. It started up
in Weimar in 1919, was driven
on to Dessau when Weimar
voted in a Nationalist state
government, and on again to
Berlin in 1929. In Berlin it came
into conflict with the Nazis and
was closed for good – that is,
until a post-war resurrection in
Chicago. The architect Walter
Gropius was its first director;
Mies van der Rohe was its last.
Painters on the staff included
Paul Klee and Vassily Kandinsky.
The work of all these seminal
figures is reflected in a changing
display.
Open: Monday and Wednesday
to Sunday 10.00–17.00hrs.

The striking Berliner Dom

◆◆◆
BERLINER DOM ✓

Museumsinsel, Map p 44–5
This Protestant cathedral and
burial place of the Hohenzollern
family was built at the turn of the
century for Kaiser Wilhelm II.
Badly damaged during World
War II, the vast High
Renaissance structure has been
restored to its original ornate
grandeur. The interior, though
splendid, is light and pleasant.
For an extreme example of
baroque decoration, see the
sarcophagi of the first Prussian
king, Friedrich and his wife
Sophie Charlotte, by Andreas
Schlüter. Evensong on Thursday
is held in English and German
and there are earphone
translations in English of the
Holy Communion service on
Sunday at 10.00hrs.

◆◆
BERLIN-MUSEUM

Lindenstrasse 14, Map p 30–1
Formerly the Supreme Court,
this grand building of 1735 was
rebuilt after World War II. The
museum, dealing with the later
centuries of Berlin's history
through models, pictures and
artefacts, is closed until 1998.
A separate Jewish Museum is
planned beside it to reflect the
contribution made by the Jewish
community to the life of the city,
reflected through photographs,
paintings and artefacts.

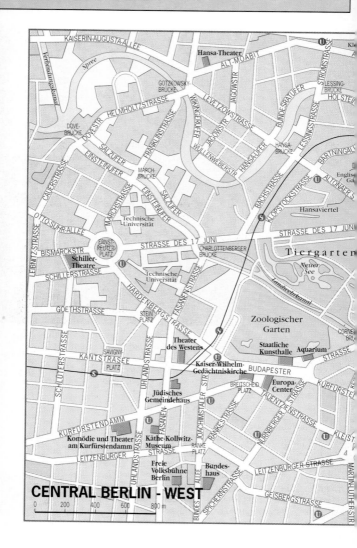

CENTRAL BERLIN - WEST

0   200   400   600   800 m

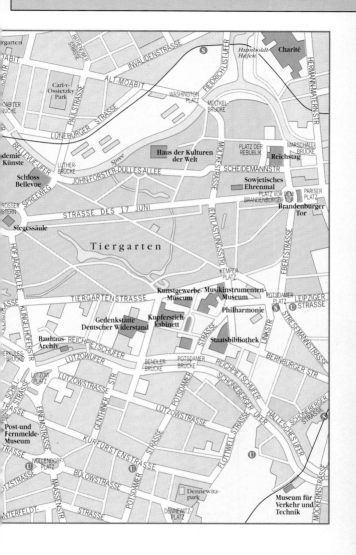

◆◆◆
BODE-MUSEUM ✓

*Am Kupfergraben –
Monbijoubrücke, Map p 44–5*
The Bode-Museum houses fine
collections of European
sculpture and a quite
astonishing display of Egyptian
antiquities (together with a fine
papyrus collection). There is
also a large and less exciting
picture gallery.
About half of the ground floor
space is taken up with sculpture
and, sometimes, chunks of the
interiors of buildings. The
Coptic collection offers quaint
stone carving. Byzantine works
include mosaics from San
Michele in Ravenna; and there is
German medieval and,

In the Botanischer Garten

particularly, 16th-century
polychrome wood sculpture, full
of emotion and character. The
Egyptian collection is also on the
ground floor. There are
mummies of adults and children,
the body of a two-year-old child
entirely turned to leather, and
mummified animals, their
skeletons revealed by X-ray.
Equally haunting are the lifelike
mummy-masks, the strange little
representations of baboons and
dogs with enormous ears.
Most of the upstairs is occupied
by paintings, worth a look but
not comparable with the
Museen Dahlem.
Open: Tuesday to Sunday
09.00–17.00hrs.

◆
BOTANISCHER GARTEN UND
BOTANISCHES MUSEUM

*Königin-Luise-Strasse 6–8,
Steglitz, Map p 10–11*
A pleasant place to spend a
couple of hours, particularly
after a session in the Dahlem
museum complex near by.
There are landscaped gardens,
wild woods, tropical houses and
greenhouses and beds of
scented herbs and flowers for
the blind. The Botanisches
Museum is by the north
entrance of the gardens.
Open: (gardens) daily in
summer 09.00–20.00hrs
(tropical houses shut at
17.15hrs); (museum) Tuesday to
Sunday 10.00–17.00hrs.

◆◆◆
BRANDENBURGER TOR ✓

Map p 44–5
Much of the history of the city
has been enacted against the

Imposing Brandenburger Tor

backdrop of this monument. The Brandenburg Gate was built in 1791 by the neo-classical architect Carl Langhans to replace an earlier baroque toll gate, and at that time marked the western boundary of Berlin. The model was the Propylaea, the entranceway to the Acropolis in Athens, with classical columns that were later surmounted by the Quadriga – a four-horse chariot – driven by the goddess of peace.
Though it was originally called the 'Gate of Peace', its associations have been rather the reverse. Napoleon, the victor at the battle of Jena, was so taken with the Quadriga that he sent it back to Paris in 1806. Following the fortunes of war, it was brought back a few years later. The Nazis organised torchlight processions to pass through this gate; and it was here in November 1989 that it became a symbol of joy as citizens began to tear the Wall down.

◆◆
BRECHT-HAUS
Chauseestrasse 125, Map p 44–5
The house where poet and playwright Bertolt Brecht spent his last years with his wife, actress Helene Weigel, has been left largely as it was when he lived in it.
Brecht abandoned Germany in 1933, finally ending up in the US. In 1948 he returned to East Berlin and set up his theatrical company, the Berliner Ensemble. His library, a plain

white-walled room with a pine
floor, is lined with books, and
with posters for the Berliner
Ensemble. After Brecht's death,
Helene Weigel lived out her
years on the ground floor. The
house is open for visits by a
guided tour at half hour
intervals. There is a basement
restaurant that serves food
cooked to Weigel's own
recipes.

The view from the library is
over the **Dorotheenstädtischer
Friedhof** (cemetery) where
Brecht, Weigel and many others
of Berlin's most celebrated
citizens are buried, including
the philosopher Georg Hegel
and Karl Friedrich Schinkel, the
architect.
Open: Tuesday, Wednesday
and Friday 10.00–12.00hrs;
Thursday 17.00–19.00hrs;
Saturday 09.30–12.00 and
12.30–14.00hrs.

◆◆
BRÖHAN-MUSEUM
Schlossstrasse la, Map p 30–1
This unexpected and pleasing
museum offers Art Nouveau and
Art Deco furniture, glass,
ceramics, silver and so on,
accompanied by many paintings
and a smaller number of
sculptures. Each gallery is a
total room, complete with period
contents from the rug on the
floor to the pictures on the walls.
Note especially the nudes by
Willy Jaeckel and the paintings
and sculpture of Jean Lambert-
Rucki; and do not miss the top-
floor display of swirling,
curvilinear Art Nouveau
silver.
Open: Tuesday to Sunday
10.00–18.00hrs.

◆
BRÜCKE MUSEUM
Bussardsteig 9, Map p 10–11
The Brücke Museum is tucked
away among pines and silver
birches on the edge of the
Grunewald in the west of the
city. Die Brücke, 'the Bridge',
was the name taken by a group
of Expressionist artists working
mainly in Dresden between 1905
and 1913. Their hallmarks were
bold simplification and striking,
often clashing, combinations of
colours. The collection changes,
but you should see work by
Ernst Ludwig Kirchner, Karl
Schmidt-Rottluff, and Emil Nolde
– all still exciting today.
Open: Wednesday to Monday
11.00–17.00hrs.

DEUTSCH-RUSSISCHES MUSEUM

Zwieseler Strasse 4, Map p 10–11

This house, home of the Red Army Command centre in the final days of World War II, was the scene of the signing of the Act of Military Surrender on 8 May 1945. Now it is a museum on the history of German-Russian relations in this century through posters, letters, photographs and uniforms. Explanations in German only. Visitors can walk through the room where the German surrender was formalised. Reached by S-Bahn to Karlshorst.

Open: Tuesday to Sunday 10.00-18.00hrs.

◆◆ DIE MAUER (THE WALL)

Map p 30–1

There are few remains of the 97 miles (155 km) of The Wall (its curious course dictated by local administrative boundaries) that once so cruelly divided the city. A half-mile (1km) stretch of it remains by the Spree on Muhlenstrasse. In 1990, following the tradition of The Wall as public art expressing local protest, selected artists, some well known, were invited to paint it with murals and graffiti. It is now known as the **East Side Gallery**.

Detail from a Wall mural

◆
EHRENMAL FÜR DIE OPFER DES 20 JULI 1944
Stauffenbergstrasse 11–14, Map p 36–7
The 20 July Memorial and Gedenkstätte Deutscher Widerstand is a memorial of German resistance against fascism within the former German Army Office (easy to

Fernsehturm, the ultimate TV aerial

miss because the signs are very modest). Claus Graf Schenk von Stauffenberg, the leader of the plot to blow up Hitler on 20 July 1944 – last of several conspiracies – was chief of staff here. Wreaths stand against a wall inscribed with the names of the conspirators. They were shot there, their execution illuminated by the headlamps of staff cars.

The failure of the assassination attempt led to a massive round-up of any possible focus of resistance to Hitler. Thousands were imprisoned, tortured and executed.

An exhibition on the second floor of the building has photographs, display notes (in German only) and contemporary documents recording the activities of the many groups within German society who refused to tolerate or ignore the outrage of National Socialism.

Open: Monday to Friday 09.00–18.00hrs; Saturday, Sunday and holidays 09.00–13.00hrs.

◆
EPHRAIMPALAIS
Poststrasse 16, Map p 44–5
This reconstructed mansion on the border of the Nikolaiviertel, now a museum, is one of the gems of former East Berlin. The original was demolished to make way for a road scheme, but the façade was kept safe in West Berlin, available for re-use when the area was restored. It houses a museum on Berlin, from the period of the Electors (starting in the 14th century) up to the 19th century, with

interesting paintings in particular.
Open: Monday 10.00–16.00hrs; Tuesday and Sunday 10.00–17.00hrs; Wednesday and Saturday 10.00–18.00hrs.

◆
EUROPA-CENTER
Map p 36–7
At the head of Tauentzienstrasse and opposite the Kaiser-Wilhelm-Gedächtniskirche, the Europa-Center is a large shopping and office complex, with cinemas, restaurants, a casino, revue and cabaret theatre as well. Ignoring the rather tacky atmosphere, visit the Verkehrsamt (tourist information office) on the ground floor and then make your way up to the observation platform on the top floor, to get a view of the city.
The Breitscheidplatz, the pedestrianised area at the base of the Europa-Center, is a busy meeting place during the day – for derelicts and beggars as well as shoppers and sightseers. In the evening, the place is noisy with buskers and stallholders, but late at night the atmosphere can become more sinister.

◆
FERNSEHTURM
Alexanderplatz S-Bahn, Map p 44–5
The silhouette of the TV tower – an immense spike with a globe impaled near the top – is an inescapable element of most views of central Berlin. Depending on crowds and visibility, it is worth making the ascent to the viewing gallery (222 yards, 203m by lift), to see

Berlin spread out below. There is a revolving café on the next floor up. Expect some construction work to be going on.
Open: 09.00–23.00hrs.

◆
FRIEDENAU FRIEDHOF
Map p 30–1
Fans of singer/actress Marlene Dietrich may wish to visit her grave in the cemetery at Friedenau, a suburb southwest of Schöneberg. It is a simple affair – just her name and dates.

◆◆
GEDENKSTÄTTE PLÖTZENSEE
Hüttigpfad, Map p 30–1
The prison of Plötzensee, now a boys' penitentiary edged by canals and allotments, holds one of Berlin's most powerful and depressing monuments. Visitors pass through the high walls at the side of the penitentiary to a small paved enclosure surrounded by trees. In the small, low building here, more than 2,500 people died. As well as those who resisted the Nazi dictatorship they included others merely suspected of a connection or many who were simply deemed unfit to live. Some execution proceedings were filmed and the films rushed to the Führer for his impatient inspection. Outside stands an urn containing a sample of soil from all the concentration camps.
Open: daily, March to September 08.00–18.00hrs; October and February 08.30–17.30hrs; November and January 09.30-16.30hrs; December 09.30-16.00hrs.

WHAT TO SEE – IN BERLIN

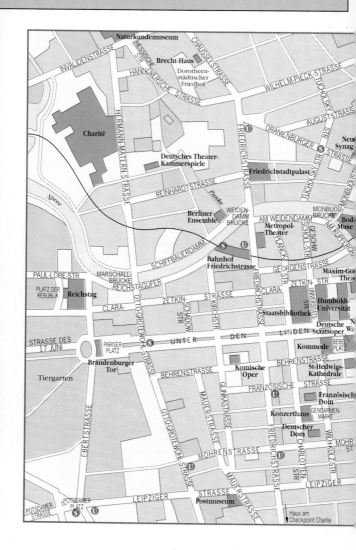

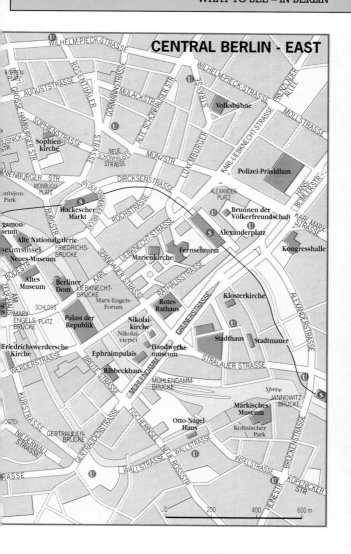

CENTRAL BERLIN - EAST

◆◆◆ GENDARMENMARKT ✓

Map p 44–5
Until its almost total obliteration in 1944, this vast square (formerly Platz der Akademie) was regarded as one of the great showpieces of Europe. Now completely restored, it is a glorious example of the post-war resurrection of Berlin, with its two cathedrals forming a kind of grand entranceway to Schinkel's Konzerthaus (formerly Schauspielhaus), one of the great 19th-century architect's finest buildings. The earlier of the two cathedrals was the Französischer Dom (French Cathedral). It was begun in 1701 for the Huguenots invited to Berlin 16 years before by the Great Elector. Today, there is a small museum of Huguenot history in the base of the tower, with the Turnstube (Tower Inn) at about fourth-floor level. Climb up further for the gallery offering fine views of the square and a wide horizon. On the far side of the square, the Deutscher Dom (German Cathedral) served the Lutheran community. It now houses the exhibition 'Fragen an die Deutsche Geschichte' (Questions about German History) – broad themes of national history from 1800 to the present day.

◆ GETHSEMANES-KIRCHE

corner of Stargarder Strasse and Greifenhager Strasse, Map p 30–1
The 19th-century brick church of Gethsemane, in Prenzlauer Berg, became a centre of peaceful protest in the run-up to the events of November 1989. It was the meeting place of the very effective pro-democracy group Neues Forum, led by the pastor of this church.

◆ GROSSER MÜGGELSEE

Map p 10–11
This large lake out to the east of the city was the main escape hatch for East Berliners after World War II and is traditionally crowded in summer. Now other Berliners have begun to use it. The approach via Friedrichshagen, with a long straight walk down the Bölschestrasse to the lakeside, has a curiously mixed atmosphere of town, country and once-prosperous lakeside villa territory. The workers at the Berliner Bürger Brau brewery, right on the water's edge among the villas, played a heroic, if ultimately doomed, role in various episodes of proletarian resistance, last against Hitler in 1933.

◆ GRUNEWALD

Map p 10–11
The Grunewald forest on the western reaches of the city, bordered by the Havel River, is a favourite recreation area for Berliners. Much of the forest, originally royal hunting woods of beech and oak, was cut down for firewood after the war. It was replanted with quick-growing species of birch and ash and still is home to a variety of wildlife including deer and wild boar (the latter safely enclosed).

Französischer Dom, Gendarmenmarkt

◆◆
HAUS AM CHECKPOINT CHARLIE

Friedrichstrasse, just off Koch Strasse, Map p 30–1
Increasingly worth a visit as traces of the Wall disappear, this is a museum dedicated to the Wall and escapology, situated just beside the now vanished Checkpoint Charlie (the former main transit point between East and West for pedestrians and motorists). It shows ingenious methods of escape used by would-be fugitives to the West – balloons, tunnels, drains and tiny vehicles with tinier secret compartments inside them. The museum may be rehoused but will remain in the area.
Open: daily 09.00–22.00hrs.

◆

HAUS DER KULTUREN DER WELT

John-Foster-Dulles-Allee, Map p 36–7

This House of World Cultures (formerly the Kongresshalle), funded by both federal and city governments, has become an important forum for 'non-European cultures and ethnic minorities', a notable exhibition space for artists, dancers, musicians, film-makers and craftspeople from the so-called 'Third World'. Lectures and weekend dances take place here.

The building was a goodwill gift from the Americans for the International Building Exhibition of 1957. It was quickly re-erected after the roof collapsed in 1980. Berliners call it the 'Pregnant Oyster'.

◆

HAVEL

Map p 10–11

Berlin is full of lakes, canals and rivers, and the Havel River forms the largest of these watery playgrounds to the west. (See **Grosser Müggelsee** for eastern lakes.) Masses of pleasure boat trips are available in summer. Boats on the Havel system may be joined at Spandau, Wannsee, Glienicke and other places.

◆◆

JAGDSCHLOSS GRUNEWALD

Grunewald, Map p 10–11

This hunting lodge deep in the woods has been taking shape since the 16th century. Many important paintings were installed here after World War II; in particular there is a splendid collection of works by Lucas Cranach the Elder (1472–1553).

The lodge is set on the banks of the Grunewaldsee, with cobbled courtyard, stables and a small hunting museum. On 3 November each year, St Hubert's Day, the exclusive riding clubs of Grunewald turn out to hunt.

Open: Tuesday to Sunday 10.00–13.00hrs; and 13.30–18.00hrs.

◆◆

JÜDISCHES GEMEINDEHAUS

Fasenenstrasse 79–80, Map p 36–7

The synagogue where the Jewish Community House now stands was burnt down on the night of 9 November 1938 – Kristallnacht or Crystal Night, the date of a fearsome onslaught against the Jews. The new building, with only the original portal of the old synagogue still standing in front, is a place of worship and meeting, and for remembrance of the millions who were killed by the Nazis. It also houses an excellent kosher restaurant.

◆◆

KAISER-WILHELM-GEDÄCHTNISKIRCHE

Breitscheidplatz, by Zoo Station, Map p 36–7

Built in 1891 as a memorial to the Kaiser, this large church was bombed in 1943. It has since been left in its ruinous condition, as a reminder of the horrors of war. Today the black and jagged remains of the original, known by Berliners as the

Broken Tooth, stand beside the shimmering blue reflection of stained glass from the new buildings flanking it.

◆◆◆
KÄTHE-KOLLWITZ-MUSEUM
Fasanenstrasse 24, Map p 36–7
An excellent collection of the work of artist, sculptor and social reformer, Käthe Kollwitz (1867–1945). Images of loss and despair predominate, and include drawings of a mother and her dying child – all the more poignant because they were done before Käthe Kollwitz's own son was killed in World War I and her only grandson in World War II. She resigned from the Prussian Academy of Art in 1933 and was forced to stop teaching and exhibiting by the Nazi government.

Käthe Kollwitz Platz is a square dedicated to the artist's memory in Prenzlauer Berg, where she lived.

Open: Wednesday to Monday 11.00–18.00hrs.

Reminder to the futility of war, the Kaiser Wilhelm Church

◆◆
KÖPENICK
*S-Bahn to Köpenick Station,
then tram, bus or 20-minute
walk, Map p 10–11*
Much of the old town of
Köpenick survives, making it
potentially one of the most
attractive spots in Berlin and its
neighbourhood. After being
extremely run down, it is now
being renovated and enjoying
some gentrification. There are
pleasant streets and a brick
town hall with *Ratskeller*
(basement restaurant), and the
whole area is interspersed with
park, river and lake.
The main attraction is the palace,
Schloss Köpenick. It houses the
overspill of the national
collection of applied art from the
Kunstgewerbe Museum in
Tiergarten (see page 52).
On entry, the first pleasure is the
wonderfully extravagant plaster
decoration of the ceiling. The
collection begins on the ground
floor and is in chronological
order, except for a
contemporary display in the
basement. Highlights include
the 'treasury', with fine gold and
silver from the 11th century; a
panelled chamber of 1548 from
Switzerland, reassembled here;
lavishly elegant 18th-century
furniture; and strangely
coloured Jugendstil (Art
Nouveau) glass, in the hallway.
Open: Wednesday to Sunday
09.00–17.00hrs, but check for
alterations.

◆◆
KREUZBERG
Map p 10–11
For an overview of this old city
district, climb the Hill of the

Cross in Viktoriapark, which at
217 feet (66m) provides a rare
high point in a generally flat
city. The somewhat
unattractive cross (1812–15) is
by Schinkel, commemorating
victories in the Napoleonic
wars. Beneath is an artificial
waterfall. Parts of western
Kreuzberg, particularly around
the handsome street of
Mehringdamm, are built on the
typical Berlin pattern of large
outward-facing city blocks with
courtyards receding within.

These, as in **Prenzlauer Berg** (see page 64) were both workplace and living quarters. The arrival of the Wall in 1961 meant that Kreuzberg was tucked away in a forgotten corner. The housing languished while intellectuals, bohemians and squatters moved in. Nowadays western Kreuzberg and its mansions are swiftly becoming gentrified, but eastern Kreuzberg retains much more of its Wall-era seediness. The

Schloss Köpenick, from the park. Built in 1681 in the Dutch baroque style, it now houses a small museum of applied art

most intensive squatting was on Oranienplatz. Here radical graffiti are still much in evidence, and all down Oranienstrasse there are alternative bars and restaurants. Cheap housing drew in Turkish 'guest-workers' and this part of the town has an Islamic air.

WHAT TO SEE – IN BERLIN

KUNSTGEWERBEMUSEUM

Tiergartenstrasse 6,
Map p 36–7

Despite an unpromising exterior, the Museum of Applied Art is one of those Berlin museums where a fine collection receives a brillliant display. It contains much of the pre-World War II national collection of applied art (the rest is in **Schloss Köpenick**), with some recent additions. Entry is along the side and up a staircase to a main foyer at the back. The collection proper starts one level below, with a fine display of crosses, stained glass, caskets and so on, from medieval to Renaissance. The sequence resumes on the top floor running from Renaissance to Art Deco. Glass and ceramics are outstanding here. The collection now carries on in the basement, coming up to date with furniture and objects of domestic use.

Open: Tuesday to Friday 09.00–17.00hrs; Saturday and Sunday 10.00–17.00hrs.

KUPFERSTICHKABINETT

Matthäikirchplatz 8,
Map p 36–7

This collection of prints, drawings and engravings, an amalgamation of the collections of the Dahlem and Museumsinsel galleries, has now found a permanent home in the Tiergarten's Kulturforum. Works by Dürer and Botticelli are among the exhibits.

Open: Tuesday to Friday 9.00–17.00, Saturday and Sunday 10.00–17.00.

KURFÜRSTENDAMM

Map p 36–7

This long avenue (two miles, 3.5km), full of shops, restaurants and pavement cafés, street stalls and entertainers, is the heart and main thoroughfare of modern Berlin – a position once enjoyed by the Alexanderplatz and Friedrichstrasse. Even the Möhring and Kranzler cafés were moved to the Ku'damm after World War II. Now it is close to the centre of communications, with Zoo Station, the bus terminus, Breitscheidplatz and the Europa-Center near by. There is a mixture of exclusive and popular shops on Ku'damm itself with smaller speciality shops in the adjoining streets. Many city tours begin and end here.

Originally this long road was merely the most direct route through the city to the royal hunting lodge at Grunewald forest in the west. It was considerably smartened up in the 19th century as a result of Bismarck's plans to make it a rival to the Champs Elysées in Paris.

LÜBARS

Map p 10–11

On the northern edge of West Berlin, Lübars is a suprisingly rural spot to find within the city limits. With cobbled country roads and riding stables, a pair of pubs, an old-fashioned village church and the oldest house in Berlin, it remains an agreeable retreat for a summer afternoon.

Märkisches Museum and Zille statue

◆
MARIA REGINA MARTYRUM
Heckerdamm 230–2,
Map p 30–1
This stark and sombre Catholic
church was built in 1963 as a
memorial to the 'martyrs to
freedom of faith and conscience
in the years 1933–1945'. Heavily
symbolic, the church was built
to face in the direction of
Plötzensee prison, scene of the
execution of many resistance
workers (see **Gedenkstätte
Plötzensee**).

The open space in front of the
church is surrounded by high
walls of basalt slabs to create
the impression of a concentration
camp yard. In the crypt there is
a most moving bronze *Pieta* by
Fritz König, and a gravestone
provides a symbolic resting
place for those executed at
Plötzensee. The church is plain
to the point of austerity, with
simple wooden benches, a large
abstract mural by Georg

Meistermann, and a tiny 14th-century Gothic Madonna and Child. Natural light filters through from concealed windows.
Open: daily 09.00–17.30hrs.

◆◆
MARIENKIRCHE
Karl-Liebknecht-Strasse 8,
Map p 44–5
Once tightly packed among surrounding houses but now in open space across from the Rotes Rathaus (Red Town Hall), the Marienkirche is a Gothic survivor of World War II right in the city centre. Built in 1262, rebuilt at the end of the 14th century and needing not much more than new windows after World War II, it is open and spacious inside, with an ornate baroque pulpit by Andreas Schlüter and plenty of elaborate memorials to the departed. A medieval wall painting, rediscovered in 1860 and now badly faded by pollution, shows a 'Dance of Death', inspired by an outbreak of the plague in 1484.

◆◆
MÄRKISCHES MUSEUM
Am Köllnischer Park 5,
Map p 44–5
This imposing fake Gothic building was founded in 1874 by the City of Berlin, and houses a city museum. There is a collection of fine glass and porcelain, earthenware and wrought ironwork, and theatrical memorabilia from the great days of Max Reinhardt. Paintings of Berlin show the city's classical buildings taking shape, and there are romantic studies of a

Marienkirche – Berlin's second oldest church

rural Kreuzberg, with more recent Berlin street scenes by Lesser Ury. Outside, a statue of Heinrich Zille shows Berlin's best-loved cartoonist sketching while a local lad peers over his shoulder. A couple of Berlin bears are kept in the small Köllnischer Park immediately behind the museum.
Open: Wednesday to Friday 09.00–17.00hrs; Saturday 09.00–18.00hrs; Sunday 10.00–18.00hrs.

◆◆◆
MARTIN-GROPIUS-BAU
Stresemannstrasse 110,
Map p 30–1
This lavish 19th-century building, one of the most spectacular in Berlin, houses a notable collection of Berlin art, and material on Jewish history (until the opening of a new Jewish Museum, planned for 1998).

The Wall used to run so close to its front door that a main entrance was established in the back. Across the road from it in Mitte there stands the former Prussian parliament, and next door again the former Nazi Air Ministry, grim and grey. Next door to the Gropius-Bau itself stood Prinz Albrechtstrasse 8, the Gestapo headquarters, also used as a postal address for those incarcerated in concentration camps. It was one of a row of buildings obliterated after World War II in an attempt to purge hateful memories. Part of

Ornate Martin-Gropius-Bau

the cellars of the headquarters is now occupied by the **Topography of Terror Museum**, showing photographs and text about the people held there. (*Open*: 10.00–18.00hrs.) Inside Martin-Gropius-Bau, the two-storeyed central space with columns in black and gold is one of Berlin's leading exhibition spaces. The paintings and sculptures of the permanent collection run from the late 19th century, through Expressionism, Dada and Constructivism into the Neue Sachlickeit (New Objectivity) which followed, then on again through World War II and up into the 1980s.

The range is very wide, from Lesser Ury street scenes to brilliant constructions by Naum Gabo. The Jewish exhibition is concerned mainly with documenting the human and cultural importance of the Jewish community. Much of the display is in written format, in German only.

Open: Tuesday to Sunday 10.00–18.00hrs (sometimes later in summer).

♦♦♦
MUSEEN DAHLEM ✓

Zehlendorf, Map p 10–11
The leafy suburbs of southwest Berlin are the setting for this prestigious museum complex, set up in 1948 as an alternative to the then Communist Humboldt University in East Berlin, and largely funded at its inception by the Henry Ford Foundation.

It is best to plan your route fairly carefully because each outstanding collection seems to run into another. Pick up a *Wegweiser* (plan) from the information desk.

The **Museum für Völkerkunde** (Ethnography Museum) covers Ancient America, including Peruvian pottery and Guatemalan sculpture; Africa, including Benin bronzes; the South Seas, including boats and houses; and Asia, including Tang ceramics and Indonesian masks and puppets. Displays change regularly.

For many the **Gemäldegalerie** (Picture Gallery) is the high point of Dahlem. The Italian rooms are marvellous, though not unique, with works by masters from Botticelli to Titian and Caravaggio. German painting is good in parts, with Cranach the Elder and Hans Holbein both featured. There is fine Spanish work from Velázquez, Zurbaran and Goya, and a strong display from the English and Scottish 18th century. But the area in which Dahlem may be the best in the world is in early Netherlandish paintings, the so-called Flemish primitives.

Room 143 offers three Van Eycks including the gem-like *Madonna in the Church*. Petrus Christi, a contemporary, offers *St Barbara* and the strange portrait of a *Young Woman*, her eyes like candle-flames laid sideways. Rogier van der Weyden, considered by some as great a master as Van Eyck, is almost entirely responsible for Room 144. The collection continues, with treasures like Ouwater's *Raising of Lazarus*, Bosch's *John on Patmos*, and Bruegel's *Netherlandish Proverbs*. Beyond this section is a notable choice of Dutch works by Vermeer and contemporaries, and a magnificent gathering of Rembrandts.

The **Skulpturengalerie** (Sculpture Gallery) has early Christian German Gothic and Italian Renaissance sculpture, in bronze, ivory, gold and wood. There is also a display of miniatures from the 16th to 18th centuries.

The museums of **Indian**, **Islamic** and **East Asian art** offer a wonderful display of the most beautiful art and artefacts – pictures, wall hangings, sculptures, carpets and tiles, individually lit against a black background.

This is a museum to come back to again and again. It also has a separate children's section, and a Museum for the Blind.

Open: Tuesday to Friday 09.00–17.00hrs; Saturday and Sunday 10.00-17.00hrs.

◆

MUSEUM FÜR DEUTSCHE VÖLKERKUNDE

Im Winkel 6, Map p 10–11

Five minutes' walk from the main Dahlem museums, this is a place to see the popular, mostly rural, culture of the German-speaking peoples of central Europe. There are some beautifully decorated chests and cradles, and folk costumes, homely domestic tools and craftwork from Swiss and Austrian as well as German sources.

Open: Tuesday to Friday 09.00–17.00hrs; Saturday and Sunday 10.00–17.00hrs.

◆◆

MUSEUM FÜR VERKEHR UND TECHNIK

Trebbinner Strasse 9, Map p 36–7

An entertaining jumble of a museum on the theme of transport and technology. Displays include huge stuffed oxen pulling a cart, light Fokker

The Dahlem Museum complex exhibits art from all periods

aircraft suspended from the ceiling, cars, buses and motorbikes and, in the old workshops of the Anhalter Bahnhof, a great collection of early trains. The technology is represented by ancient domestic appliances, early typewriters, and modern computers, paper presses and weaving looms. Anything that can withstand the curious touch of young children is available for hands-on treatment.
Open: Tuesday to Friday 09.00–17.30hrs; Saturday and Sunday 10.00-1800hrs.

◆◆
MUSIKINSTRUMENTEN-MUSEUM
Tiergartenstrasse 1,
Map p 36–7
A light and cheerful museum on two floors, it houses a collection of musical instruments from the 16th century to the present day, including ancient bagpipes and the latest electronic instruments. It is a bonus if your visit coincides with a demonstration of a particular instrument. In the basement there is a café-bar and a small stage. Guided tours on Saturday at 11.00, followed

Outside the Neue Nationalgalerie

years, and forms part of the Cultural Complex running south from the Potsdamer Platz end of the Tiergarten. It includes the **Kunstgewerbemuseum**, **Musikinstrumenten-Museum**, and **Staatsbibliothek** (see separate entries), and the **Philharmonie** concert hall. The Neue Nationalgalerie now houses German and international paintings from the 20th century, with works by the likes of Max Ernst, Oskar Kokoschka, Edvard Munch, John Cage and Anselm Kiefer. A new museum of contemporary painting is planned to open in the old Hamburger Bahnhof station in 1996.
Open: Tuesday to Friday 09.00–17.00hrs; Saturday and Sunday 10.00–17.00hrs.

by a half-hour concert on the Wurlitzer organ at noon.
Open: Tuesday to Friday 09.00–17.00hrs; Saturday and Sunday 10.00–17.00hrs.

◆◆◆
NEUE NATIONALGALERIE
Potsdamer Strasse 50,
Map p 30–1
Mies van der Rohe designed this airy pavilion in glass and steel (built 1965–8). It was his last commission for a city from which he was exiled for many

◆◆◆
NEUE SYNAGOGE ✓

Oranienburger Strasse 30, Mitte.
Map p 44–5
The brilliant Moorish dome of this synagogue is a dramatic addition to the Berlin skyline. The original was built in 1866 in this traditionally Jewish area of Scheunenviertel. It was damaged in the fires of Kristallnacht in 1939. Though the interior was gutted by Allied bombs in 1945, the façade remained standing. It was re-opened in May 1995, not as a working synagogue, but as a museum and a memorial as well as a study and research centre. Information is in English and German.
Open: Sunday to Friday 10.00-18.00hrs; closed Saturday and Jewish holidays.

NEUE WACHE

Unter den Linden, Map p 44–5
Schinkel's New Guard House,
with more than a touch of the
Greek temple, appears in many
19th-century paintings, with
soldiers lounging elegantly
against its Doric columns.

Originally built as a guardhouse
for the Royal Palace, after World
War II it was decided to make the
Neue Wache a monument to anti-
militarism and anti-fascism. Now
it is a memorial to the victims of

*Nikolaiviertel, where modern
architecture recalls pre-war style*

war and tyranny. A bronze sculpture of the mother with her dead son, an enlarged version of an original by Käthe Kollwitz, stands alone in the middle of this otherwise empty austere space.

NIKOLAIKIRCHE
Nikolaiviertel, Map p 44–5
This twin-towered church stands at the heart of the Nikolaiviertel district, which is named after it. Some of the lower level is original but most of the remainder, lofty as it is, is reconstructed. The church houses an extension of the **Märkisches Museum** (see page 54), with models showing the development of Berlin and Neu-Kölln as medieval river settlements. It also has medieval artefacts and sculptures, and a great many florid baroque memorials. Outside, there is a fountain with the Berlin bear.
Open: Tuesday to Sunday 10.00–18.00hrs.

NIKOLAIVIERTEL
Map p 44–5
This entirely rebuilt area lies between the Rotes Rathaus and the Spree. It provides interesting streets to wander in, shops, pubs, restaurants, a good museum (the **Ephraimpalais**), and more atmosphere than might be anticipated.

OLYMPIASTADION
Map p 10–11
The 'Reich sport centre' was built for the 11th summer Olympics (1936) by Werner March. This was an occasion to show the world the achievements of the chief city of Nazi Germany. But when the black athlete Jesse Owens won four gold medals, denting the notion of Aryan superiority, Hitler left his place on the podium in disgust. The stadium is still used for all sorts of sporting and musical events.

OTTO-NAGEL-HAUS
Märkisches Ufer, Map p 44–5
This small museum-gallery is in one of the well-restored 18th-century mansions on the Märkisches Ufer, in the heart of fomer East Berlin. Many of the works are by Otto Nagel (1894–1967) who became much admired by the GDR. In the 1920s he was painting dark grey, powerfully miserable scenes of proletarian life. By the early 1940s, despite the war, his palette had lightened and his Berlin street scenes became actually pretty. There is also outstanding small-scale sculpture by Käthe Kollwitz and Theo Balden. Painters to note include the sardonically watchful Hans Grundig (1901–58) and Conrad Felixmuller (1897–1977).
Open: Tuesday to Sunday 09.00–17.00hrs.

◆◆◆ PERGAMON-MUSEUM ✓

Museumsinsel, Map p 44–5
Traditionally the most prestigious museum in Berlin, the Pergamon is the fruit of imperial purchase and plunder on an epic scale. It contains two of the most remarkable buildings of the ancient world,

and is a marvellous but foot-wearying place. If possible, it is best to make several short visits. The **architectural display** is on the ground floor. First on entry is the altar from the ancient Greek and Roman city of Pergamon (now in Turkey), round which the whole museum is built. It is vast, with the widest of marble stairways ascending towards a low but very wide pillared portal. All round the base (and the rest of the gallery) run huge sculpted friezes.

To the left there is a Hellenistic room, with more from Pergamon and immense columns from elsewhere. In a gallery to the right is the astoundingly elaborate – and

Pergamon-Museum's stern façade

beautiful – Roman gateway to the market at Miletus. Pass through this room to the right and you will encounter an even greater surprise – the whole of the Ishtar Gate of Babylon, built during the reign of Nebuchadnezzar II (604–562BC). Stretching away from the gate runs the processional way of Ancient Babylon, full of tooth-gnashing lions. This is the heart of the **West Asiatic collection**.

The **East Asian collection** is on the top floor in the wing to the left as you face the building. Among other things, it takes the visitor on a chronological tour of Chinese porcelain.

Architecture apart, the major element of the **Greek and Roman antiquities** is sculpture, running from archaic through classical Greek to Roman, and ending with carved tombs and urns of the greatest bea;uty and elaboration.

Upstairs is the **Islamic collection** which some think the finest of them all. It includes not merely the extraordinary carved façade of the castle of Mshatta in Jordan but also a huge range of smaller artefacts – carpets, glass and wooden inlays, tiled prayer-niches from mosques, an amazing panelled room from a private house in Aleppo, Indian miniatures and so on through a range of treasures.

The **Ethnography Museum** is different in scale, style and intent. Hidden away in the basement under Greek and Roman sculpture, a small gallery shows arts and crafts with nice objects in wood particularly, and then moves on, via an anti-

Aboard the ferry boat to Pfaueninsel (Peacock Island)

fascist section on the Jews, to a display of Berlin costume.
Open: daily 09.00–18.00hrs (Friday 10.00–18.00hrs). Only parts of the museum are open on Monday and Tuesday. These include the major architectural exhibits on the ground floor.

◆◆
PFAUENINSEL
Map p 10–11
'Peacock Island' is a nature reserve linked to the Glienicke Park/Berliner Forest by a regular ferry service across the Havel. It was used by Friedrich Wilhelm II as a romantic hidey-hole for himself and his mistress, Countess Wilhelmine von Lichtenau. Here he built a mock ruin, the Schloss Pfaueninsel – of limited interest except for the existence (rare for Berlin) of the original furniture and decoration, wallpapers, paintings and loos.

The island was filled with exotic creatures, but only peacocks remained by 1842. Now, it is a popular leisure spot for Berliners. This is a 'no smoking, no dogs and no music' island.

◆◆
POTSDAMER PLATZ
Map p 44–5
It is said that more traffic passed through the Potsdamer Platz in the 1920s and 1930s than through any other city square in Europe. Berlin's first traffic light was here. It was bombed flat during World War II, then after the Wall went up the former busy hub became famous for its ghostly emptiness. Today the traffic is moving again but around a mess of construction sites. Pedestrians may find the area hard to negotiate until most building is complete. Although

some companies who were initially enthusiastic to site their businesses here have withdrawn and there have been long wrangles over the use and style of new buildings, the work continues apace.

Join a walking tour to stroll on the site of Hitler's Chancery or speculate on the position of the bunker where he killed himself. Berlin Walks runs tours in English (contact the tourist office for details).

PRENZLAUER BERG
Map p 30–1
Prenzlauer Berg, particularly the part lying just east of Schönhauser Allee, has more to offer than any other district in the east of the city except for Mitte and possibly Köpenick. It was a teeming 19th-century residential and manufacturing district, built on the typical Berlin pattern of imposing façades giving way to a series of courtyards. Though still in general very run down, its potential is revealed by the streets that have been done up, (like Husemannstrasse) and the busy café and street life growing up around them. A Käthe Kollwitz bronze of herself in the square named after her, watches over the children of the district where she lived.

RATHAUS SCHÖNEBERG
Martin-Luther-Strasse,
Map p 30–1
Schöneberg Town Hall was the seat of government for West Berlin after 1948. From its balcony, President John F

Kennedy made his speech of support for the people of West Berlin in 1963 in which he declared, 'Ich bin ein Berliner' – 'I am a Berliner'. The bell that rings at noon each day from the top of the tower is a copy of the Liberty Bell in Philadelphia, and was donated by Americans in 1950.

REICHSTAG
Platz der Republik,
Map p 36–7
No building in Berlin evokes the drama of recent German history more clearly than the German Parliament. It was built in 1884–94 from war reparations exacted from the French after the Franco-Prussian war; the

The battle-scarred Reichstag

new Republic was announced from its balcony in 1918; and it was the burning of the Reichstag in 1933 which provided the excuse for Hitler's unchallenged assumption of dictatorial powers. In the last days of the Reich, these rooms and corridors were the scene for the final battle between Soviet forces and the defending SS troops.

The German parliament will eventually return to this site and to a new Bundestag designed by the British architect, Sir Norman Foster. Construction work on this and other projects, which include government offices and a Holocaust memorial, will last until the end of the decade. Meanwhile the Reischstag is closed to the public.

ROTES RATHAUS
Alexanderplatz, Map p 44–5
After a spell as town hall of East Berlin alone, this splendid brick building – nicknamed for its colour, not its politics – has been restored as the seat of the mayor of a unified Berlin. Built in 1861–9 and rebuilt after the war, it is decorated with a terracotta frieze, the 'Berlin Chronicle'.

◆◆
SCHEUNENVIERTEL
Mitte, Map p 44–5
This old Jewish and working-class district just behind Alexanderplatz is now the cutting edge of 'alternative' culture in Berlin. Blackened tenements conceal a hive of theatre and cabaret groups, dance and music studios, bars and cafés. Tacheles, on Oranienburger Strasse, is a warren of workshops and studios with a backyard full of ironwork sculpture. In Grosser Hamburger Strasse, relics of Jewish history include the New Synagogue (see page 59), a memorial on the site of an old people's home which was a collection centre for Jews before deportation to concentration camps, and the 'Missing House', an empty bombed space with plaques on neighbouring houses bearing the names of its former residents. Restored Sophienstrasse is an example of how it might all look one day.

◆
SCHLOSS BELLEVUE
Spreeweg, Map p 36–7
This summer place in Tiergarten was originally built for the

younger brother of Frederick the Great in 1785. It was completely rebuilt after World War II. Now it is the official residence of the President of the Federal Republic of Germany.

◆◆
SCHLOSS CHARLOTTENBURG
Luisenplatz, Map p 30–1
Schloss Charlottenburg, the one major Prussian palace still to be seen in the city, was built as a small summer palace for the future Queen Sophie Charlotte in 1695, in what was then a rural retreat. It was later enlarged, and now offers three main areas to visit. These are the Royal Apartments; the Knobelsdorff Wing (with more royal rooms, plus pictures); and the palace park (with three smaller buildings to see). For tours (in German) of the **Royal Apartments**, cross the courtyard by Andreas Schlüter's much admired equestrian statue of the Great Elector, and enter to the left of the main door. Visitors are led through increasingly grand baroque rooms built in imitation of the French royal style. The finest is the Ovale Saal, with tall windows, gilt and carving. The Porzellankabinett (porcelain room) reveals a taste for chinoiserie gone mad, and the chapel has a painted ceiling portraying the Virgin, looking like Sophie Charlotte. The **Knobelsdorff Wing** has rooms containing paintings from the National Gallery's Romantic collection. On the right you will find the hyper-real, hyper-romantic pictures of Caspar David Friedrich (1774–1840),

depicting everything from mauve mist on mountain tops to solitary figures brooding by storm-swept seas. There are also powerful works by the Berlin architect Karl Friedrich Schinkel. Some show vast, fantastical Gothic churches, others are drawn from Ancient Greece. Other ground-floor rooms show 19th-century palace décor and furniture, along with portraits, and Berlin cityscapes.

Once-rural Schloss Charlottenburg

Up on the first floor, blinding in its new gilt, is the reconstructed **Golden Gallery**, built for Frederick the Great. His apartments at the far end of the Knobelsdorff Wing contain a number of paintings by the French rococo artist Watteau. Immediately behind the palace is a formal, baroque garden, surrounded by the informal **palace park**. There are three buildings in the park which all deserve a call. The **Schinkel Pavilion** is charming inside. It was built in 1825 as a summerhouse for Friedrich Wilhelm III, and stands just round the far corner of the Knobelsdorff Wing. Downstairs, note the set of green KPM (Royal Porcelain Factory) china, with Iron Cross; upstairs, the paintings stand out, with another Gothic cathedral fantasy by Schinkel.

China in the Belvedere

Pretty in pale green, with white columns and dome, the **Belvedere** lies further back in the park and close to the canal. Once used for taking tea, it is now a porcelain museum.

The small Doric temple on the west side of the park is the **Mausoleum**. It was completed in the early 19th century for Queen Luise, wife of Friedrich Wilhelm III who was also buried here. Princes, Kaisers and their spouses followed till the end of the century. (*Closed*: November to March.)

Open: Tuesday to Friday 09.00–17.00hrs; Saturday and Sunday 10.00–17.00hrs.

◆◆
SCHLOSS GLIENICKE
Wannsee, Map P 10–11

The painter and architect Karl Friedrich Schinkel built this little Italianate pleasure palace in 1826. The palace itself is closed to the public, but the gardens are open and form one of the prettiest corners of Berlin. The front of the palace faces on to the main Berlin-Potsdam road at the Glienicker Brücke (bridge), former border point between East and West and site of dramatic spy exchanges. The back of the palace looks out past columns, pavilions and huge beech trees, to open lake and sky, with the view of the fake ruins of Frederick the Great's Sanssouci (see page 82) beyond. Fragments of romantic stonework from elsewhere are built into the courtyard walls at the rear of the main building, and there is a particularly pretty rotunda overlooking the bridge.

The **Volkspark Klein-Glienicke** is a landscaped park running back from Glienicke Palace towards the **Pfaueninsel** (see page 62). Berliners flock here on summer weekends, filling the car parks. There is a lakeside trail through woods to the small Russian church of Nikolskoe, complete with onion dome. This was built for Tsar Nikolas of Russia by his father-in-law, Friedrich Wilhelm III. Russian-style log-cabin restaurants serve meals and drinks, and the ferry point to the Pfaueninsel is within easy walking distance. Boats depart from Glienicke to all principal destinations on the lakes.

◆◆◆
SIEGESSÄULE

Strasse des 17 Juni, Map p 30–1
The Victory Column stands in
the 'Grosser Stern' (Great Star)
Square in Strasse des 17 Juni.
Perched at a height of 220 feet
(67m) the golden winged
creature on top, holding aloft a
victory garland, is a landmark
for miles around. The column
commemorates successful wars
against Denmark, Austria and
France, and is adorned with the

Siegessäule, an eye-catching sight

barrels of captured cannon.
Mosaics at the base celebrate
the achievement of German
unity. Others (now removed)
showed military conquests.
Climb the spiral staircase for
fine city views.
Strasse des 17 Juni is named
after the day in 1953, when
Soviet tanks were sent in to
crush a popular uprising in
East Berlin.
Open: Easter to October,
Tuesday to Sunday
09.00–18.00hrs; Monday
13.00–17.30hrs.

◆◆
SOWJETISCHES EHRENMAL
Strasse des 17 Juni, Map p 36–7
The heroic bronze of a Soviet
soldier in greatcoat and helmet
stands as a memorial to the
many thousands of Soviet
soldiers who died in the battle
for Berlin in the last days of the
war. The two tanks flanking him
are said to be the first to reach

*Berliners' favourite park, the
Tiergarten*

the city in 1945; the surrounding
márble was taken from Hitler's
headquarters.
The Soviet Memorial stands
within former West Berlin, but
was guarded until reunification
by young Soviet soldiers. A few
yards away, the statue of Der
Rufer – the Caller – faces east
and calls for peace.

◆
SPANDAU
Map p 10–11
The moated citadel of Spandau
and the Old Town at the
confluence of the rivers Spree
and Havel make a pleasant out-
of-centre visit. Spandau Gaol,
however, which for many years
contained Hitler's deputy Rudolf
Hess as its sole inmate, was
obliterated after his death in
1987.
The 16th-century **Zitadelle**,
handsome in reddish brick,
stands on the site of an early
castle. It protected Berlin from
the northwest and acted as a
checkpoint for river access.
Above the main gateway is a
museum with war machinery
and other curiosities from the
Middle Ages. The oldest part of
the fortress is the crenellated
Juliusturm, or Julius Tower
(strictly for the energetic). This
gives fine views of fortress, river
and moat.
Open: Tuesday to Friday
09.00–17.00hrs; Saturday and
Sunday 10.00–17.00hrs.
Though largely reconstructed,
Spandau **Old Town** is made
agreeable by its pedestrian
precinct, tall brick church and a
number of half-timbered
buildings, some of them genuine
survivors.

Spandau's citadel across the moat

STAATSBIBLIOTHEK

Potsdamer Strasse 33,
Map p 36–7
Designed by Hans Scharoun,
along with the Philharmonie
across the road, this is one of the
most modern and best-stocked
libraries in Europe, open to all
and much used by students.
Racks of international
newspapers are kept in the
entrance hall. Frequent
exhibitions and chamber
concerts are held in the Otto
Braun Saal.
Open: Monday to Friday
09.00–21.00hrs; Saturday
09.00–17.00hrs.

TEMPELHOF
LUFTBRÜCKENDENKMAL

Tempelhof, Map p 30–1

The Airlift Memorial consists of
three arcs shooting westwards
into the sky at the entrance to
Tempelhof airport. They
symbolise the three air
corridors which kept the city
supplied with essentials during
the Berlin Blockade of 1948/9 –
including all the material
required to build Spandau
power station. The memorial is
dedicated to the 77 airmen and
groundcrew who died when
aircraft crashed during attempts
to land.

TIERGARTEN

Map p 36–7
Tiergarten, the wooded
parkland in the middle of Berlin,
literally means 'animal garden'.

Until the beginning of the 18th century it was a hunting reserve of wild boar and deer for the use of the Electors. It was devastated in World War II, but has been tidied and replanted, and is once again becoming an important recreation area for Berliners. The most pleasant area for walking is along the canal banks and round the Neuer See behind the Zoo.

◆◆
TREPTOWER PARK
Map p 10–11
Five thousand Soviet soldiers, killed in the last days of the Battle of Berlin in 1945, are buried in the memorial ground of this park. The statue of a grieving mother stands at one end of a long avenue, and the Sowjetisches Ehrenmal (see page 70) at the other. In a chamber below, mosaics depict grieving Soviet citizenry among a profusion of flowers. This park is used by strollers and cyclists. Wedding couples still come here to be photographed.

◆◆◆
UNTER DEN LINDEN AND MUSEUMSINSEL ✓

Map p 44–5
Unter den Linden is the processional way from the Brandenburg Gate to Museumsinsel on the Spree. Knocked about by time and World War II, it is lined by some of the grandest buildings in Berlin, most of them reconstructions. Under the impetus of reunification, new buildings are going up and old ones being knocked down.

Parts of this great avenue will resemble a building site for some time to come but it is still worth walking the full length of it.

Starting at the Brandenburg Gate (see **Brandenburger Tor**, page 38), you first arrive at Pariser Platz (Paris Square). Before the Wall came down, the Pariser Platz was out of bounds. Now, buses stream through, visitors gaze and hawkers sell cheap T-shirts, Russian dolls and Soviet army hats and badges. Portakabins litter the base of huge building enterprises like the new 5-star Adlon Hotel, to replace the original destroyed in 1945. The avenue itself is 200 feet (61m) across, replanted

with four rows of fragrant and now quite vigorous lime trees. On the right is the enormous former Soviet embassy, now the embassy of Russia and Ukraine. Lenin's bust has been boxed in, pending a final decision on its future.

In the next block, still to the right, the **Komische Oper**, or Comic Opera, has its offices (the theatre is behind), with a constantly running video of past performances.

Friedrichstrasse now crosses Unter den Linden. It was at the corner of Friedrichstrasse that first a whistle and then a trumpet were used to control the incredible volume of traffic at the start of the century and from

here, Unter den Linden was lined with cafés, restaurants, shops and luxury hotels. And so it will be again. The **Grand Hotel**, Berlin's classiest accommodation, stands on the right.

After just one more block, the grand old buildings of Prussian history begin, some battle scarred, others entirely rebuilt, many very recently. Some are full of the heavy, militaristic aspiration of the 1890s and 1900s. Others reach back into a more graceful age, though almost all are rather stark. First building in the grander

Crossing the Spree, from Unter den Linden to Museumsinsel

Under the lime trees (Unter den Linden)

sequence is on the left, the **Staatsbibliothek** (National Library, 1903–14). Dark and threatening on a winter evening, its many bullet holes have been patched with lighter-coloured stone. Next on the left comes **Humboldt University**. Designed by Knobelsdorff, it was originally the palace of Frederick the Great's younger brother. Statues and urns along the skyline are a dominant feature of the whole of this part of the street. In front of the university, two statues represent the brilliant Humboldt brothers, the naturalist and explorer Alexander, and Wilhelm, who founded the university. Frederick the Great, in tricorn hat, sits astride his horse in the middle of the road. The wide open space is the **Bebelplatz** (its modern name celebrates a 19th-century Socialist activist), once the Opernplatz, scene of the Nazi book-burning in May 1933. The big building beside it is called the **Kommode** or Chest of Drawers, because of the inverse curve of its handsome façade. Bang in the middle of this square, with no marker to reveal its presence, is an underground room, seen through a square of glass. The room, or library, is lined with empty bookshelves, a memorial of the 1933 book-burning, created by the Israeli artist, Micha Ullman. Down at the far end of the Bebelplatz is **St Hedwig's Cathedral**, a pleasing little structure with an outsize dome. Back on the corner of Unter den Linden, more or less in front of Frederick, is the **Deutsche Staatsoper** (State Opera) commissioned by Frederick and designed by Knobelsdorff. Still on the right-hand side, beyond the opera house and after an open space with grass and trees, comes the **Operncafé**, originally part of a string of palaces. This and the stark, white Foreign Ministry of the former GDR, bring the right-hand side of the Unter den Linden to an end. The real climax comes on the left: see separate entries for the **Neue Wache** (see page 60) and the **Zeughaus** (see page 77), the finest building on Unter den Linden. **Museumsinsel** is reached from Unter den Linden by a bridge with three Schinkel statues to either side. To your left is an open space with trees (the Lustgarten or Pleasure Garden), with the **Berliner Dom**, the city's main cathedral, on the far side, (see page 35). Behind the Lustgarten to the left are crammed the majority of Berlin's great museums (always

excluding the Dahlem complex in the West). See separate entries for the **Altes Museum** (see page 34), the **Alte Nationalgalerie** (see page 33), the **Pergamon-Museum** (see page 61) and **Bode-Museum** (see page 38); also here is the Neues-Museum, which still stands in ruins.

To the right of the bridge, the scene consists mainly of an enormous, barren square, which, together with the former Lustgarten, comprises the Schloss Platz. The copper-coloured glass building confronting the Dom is the Palast der Republik (soon to be demolished). East Germany was ruled from here until its recent dissolution. In 1918, Karl Liebknecht proclaimed a Socialist Republic from the balcony of a former royal palace on this spot. The balcony is incorporated in the Staatsratsgebäude (the State Council Building) on the south side of Schloss Platz.

WANNSEE

Map p 10–11

A great summertime destination for Berliners, the Wannsee offers sandy beaches, watersports and lakeside walks. There are two lakes, the Grosser and the Kleiner (the Great and the Little) Wannsee, which empty into the Havel River. On the shores, gracious residential suburbs have large villas surrounded by gardens, with sailing and rowing clubs dotted in between. Beside one of these boat clubs lies the grave of Heinrich von Kleist (1777–1811), the tormented

WHAT TO SEE – IN BERLIN

writer of extraordinary plays and short stories. The grave is a few steps from Bismarckstrasse, close to the Wannsee S-Bahn.

◆

WEISSENSEE FRIEDHOF
Map p 30–1
The Weissensee Friedhof is a vast Jewish cemetery in the northeast of the city, not so far from the city centre, but with sloping woods, and birdsong ringing among the dense-packed gravestones. Behind the cemetery buildings, on the right-hand side, a row of honour celebrates famous leaders of the Jewish community, among them the Berlin painter Lesser Ury (1861–1931). There is also a memorial to the resistance group led by Herbert Baum, all aged between 19 and 40, rounded up, tortured and executed in 1942–3. Here, more than anywhere, one senses the grievous loss to Berlin with the virtual extinction of its Jewish community. Men should wear hats or other head-covering.

Wannsee, a watery playground

Heads of dying warriors adorn the Zeughaus courtyard

◆◆◆ ZEUGHAUS ✓

Unter den Linden 2, Map p 44–5
This palatial baroque building began its life as a store for weapons and arms. It was completed in 1706 and is one of the oldest buildings on Unter den Linden.
The central courtyard is called the Schlüterhof, after the 22 magnificent heads of dying warriors sculpted by Andreas Schlüter. It is home to the **Museum für Deutsche Geschichte** (German History Museum), which provides a fascinating skip through the ages with an assortment of armour, manuscripts, furniture, posters, speeches and newsreels.
Open: Thursday to Tuesday 10.00–18.00hrs.

◆ ZOOLOGISCHER GARTEN

entry via Budapester Strasse or from Zoo Station (Hardenbergplatz)
Map p 30–1
This is a pleasant and well kept zoo in the centre of town. The nocturnal animal house and the aquarium (separate entrance fee) are the greatest attractions.
Open: 09.00–19.00hrs.

POSTDAM AND SANSSOUCI

One of the best reasons for visiting Berlin is to go a little further and take in Potsdam too. This fascinating town and palace complex, on the extreme southwest periphery of Berlin, is packed with memories of Frederick the Great, whose elegant Schloss Sanssouci (Sanssouci Palace) is the main reason for a visit. In this century Potsdam has seen the rise of the great Babelsberg studios where many famous German films were made; the town also gave its name to the 1945 Potsdam Conference, at which the victorious Allies decided the shape of Europe. It lies just behind the southernmost point of the Wannsee among its own little group of Brandenburg lakes and hills.

Park Sanssouci

Frederick the Great's Sanssouci Schloss stands in Park Sanssouci, a 717-acre (290-hectare) tract of hill and valley on the western edge of Potsdam. The whole of this is studded with palaces, villas, 'romantic' ruins, orangeries and

Cecilienhof, a Prussian mock-Tudor mansion, was an imperial retreat

gardens of various kinds, and is delightful to wander in. Besides the places described in the entries below, there are others worth a look if you have time. Best, and earliest, is the Chinese teahouse (1754–7), topped by a mandarin under a parasol. Closer to the park entrance is the Friedenskirche or Peace Church (1845). Schloss Charlottenhof (1826) is a small palace in villa style, and the Römische Bäder (Roman Baths) of 1826–9 is another villa in Italianate style. There is an enormous orangery (1851–60) near the Neue Kammern, and other buildings in this area include an ancient mill and the pretty, four-level Drachenhaus (dragon-house) of 1770, based on the pagoda at Kew Gardens in London.

WHAT TO SEE

CECILIENHOF
north of Potsdam
This fine half-timbered building set by a lakeside was the venue for the Potsdam Conference of 1945, where Germany's post-war future was decided, and is much visited for that reason. Part of it is a hotel.
Though it is rather too far to walk from Potsdam town, the Cecilienhof is clearly signposted from there. It was completed for the Prussian ruling Hohenzollern family in 1916 in imitation of an English Tudor mansion, and is shown to the public as it was at the time of the Conference. Stress is laid on the enormous loss of life suffered during World War II.

Visitors see the high hall where the delegations met – and the comfortable sitting room-libraries used by each team for preparation and study.
Open: daily 09.00–17.00hrs.
Closed: second and fourth Monday of each month.

NEUES PALAIS
Park Sanssouci
After the exquisite quality of Sanssouci Palace (see page 82), the New Palace of 1763–9, designed by Johann Gottfried Büring and Heinrich Ludwig Manger, may well seem crude. It too was built by Frederick the Great, however, both to house his guests and to assert, at terrifying cost, that his exhausted nation was not in fact exhausted by the Seven Years War which had come to an end in 1762.
Visitors pass from the grey vestibule into a shell-clad chamber, like an enormous, indoor grotto. After this comes what seems an infinity of ornate rooms, with court paintings and portraits. The tour concludes in the vast Marble Hall above the grotto, which was so heavy that the floor sagged when it was constructed, necessitating the speedy installation of supporting shellclad arches below.
There is a pretty palace theatre (not shown on the tour) where concerts and plays are performed. Do not miss the palace café, around from the ticket office. You ring a bell for admittance and take your cream cakes amid rococo splendours.
Open: as Schloss Sanssouci.

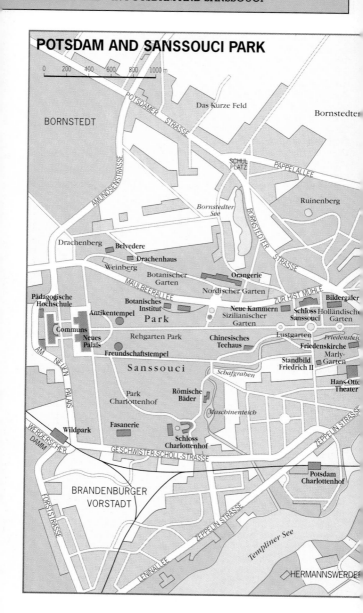

POTSDAM AND SANSSOUCI PARK

0   200   400   600   800   1000 m

BORNSTEDT

POTSDAMER STRASSE

Das Kurze Feld

Bornstedter

AMUNDSENSTRASSE

SCHUL PLATZ

PAPPELALLEE

Bornstedter See

BORNSTEDTER STRASSE

Ruinenberg

Drachenberg   Belvedere

Drachenhaus

Weinberg

Botanischer Garten

MAULBEERALLEE

Orangerie

Nordischer Garten

ZUR HIST MÜHLE

Bildergaler

Pädagogische Hochschule

Botanisches Institut

Park

Antikentempel

Neue Kammern

Sizilianischer Garten

Schloss Hollandische Sanssouci Garten

Communs

Neues Palais

Rehgarten Park

Chinesisches Teehaus

Lustgarten

Friedensteid

Friedenskirche

Freundschaftstempel

Standbild Friedrich II

Marly-Garten

AM NEUEN PALAIS

Sanssouci

Schafgraben

Hans-Otto Theater

Park Charlottenhof

Römische Bäder

Maschinenteich

ZEPPELIN STRASSE

Wildpark

Fasanerie

Schloss Charlottenhof

WERDERSCHER DAMM

GESCHWISTER-SCHOLL-STRASSE

Potsdam Charlottenhof

BRANDENBURGER VORSTADT

FORSTSTRASSE

ZEPPELIN STRASSE

Templiner See

LENINALLEE

HERMANNSWERDER

◆◆
POTSDAM

A British air raid, unleashed 200 years to the day after the foundation of Sanssouci, destroyed the centre of Potsdam, but several important buildings still survive – among them the restored Nikolaikirche (St Nicholas Church) by Schinkel. In addition, there is a considerable quantity of 18th-century housing, thoroughly pleasing where restored. The red-brick and gabled Dutch Quarter was built between 1732 and 1752 to house Dutch textile workers and is now under restoration.

Closer to the Cecilienhof, there is an area of ample log houses in Russian style, built for the retinue of the various tsars who married into the Prussian ruling family.

◆◆◆
SCHLOSS SANSSOUCI ✓

Park Sanssouci

What Frederick first intended was a summer palace where he could indulge in a life of letters and the arts *sans souci* – without care – while continuing the incessant administrative work that got him out of bed each day at 4am. He was already distanced from his wife, who never saw Sanssouci. Frederick made the initial sketch himself and this was bodied out by the architect Georg Wenzeslaus Knobelsdorff (1699–1753).

Their collaboration resulted in one of the greatest triumphs of German rococo. Sadly, it ended two years later in a dispute over Frederick's insistence on the omission of a basement. This

WHAT TO SEE – IN POTSDAM AND SANSSOUCI

The exquisite Schloss Sanssouci

terminated Knobelsdorff's career.

The success of Sanssouci derives from its human scale allied to the greatest delicacy of decoration. The building is one storey only, and is best seen from the front. It stands at the top of a hillside, terraced for vines, leading down to a fountain and statuary. This view was planned by Frederick. The back of the building, where visitors enter, is ringed by a semi-circular colonnade, with a view of dramatically composed mock-ruins on the hill opposite. Visitors are taken round in groups, on a tour (in German only) which lasts about 40 minutes. First everyone puts on large felt slippers, then shuffles into the entrance hall to admire a graceful ceiling painting by the Swede J Harper. A gallery to the left contains elegant paintings by pupils of Watteau. Note the bust of Frederick taken from his deathmask, revealing a face which is narrow, bony, quizzical and alert. His circular library is wood panelled under a sunburst ceiling, with fine bookcases in gilt and cedar. In the large adjoining chamber, divided by a pair of columns, look out for the portrait of Frederick in a blue tunic, painted by Knobelsdorff. Next comes Frederick's music room, the ornate chamber where concerts were held each evening, with Frederick himself playing the flute, as often as not his own compositions. (He composed in the mornings, on a spinet, while having his hair attended to.) The whole wall surface of the music room is covered in an extraordinary filigree of rococo gilt. Johann Sebastian Bach visited Frederick in 1747; his son, Carl Philipp Emanuel Bach, who was for a period in residence, played concerts with the king.

Among other rooms visited on the tour are the formal dining room beneath the dome, with plentiful marble and emblems of the arts, and a series of guest rooms, one decorated with wood carvings of parrots, a monkey and trails of flowers. One or other of these rooms (accounts vary) was occupied for long periods by Voltaire, the French philosopher, originally hero-worshipped by Frederick, but later teased to the point of maltreatment.

The **Bildergalerie** (picture gallery) is on the right as you face the palace from the terraces. It was built by Büring, who also designed the Chinese teahouse, and contains mainly Renaissance and baroque paintings (*open*: summer only, 09.00–17.00hrs).

The **Dutch Gardens** lie below the terrace here. On the left of the palace, the **Neue Kammern** (New Chambers) were built as an orangery in 1747, and later converted into highly decorated guestrooms (*open*: as Schloss Sanssouci, but closed Fridays). Beneath, on the righthand side as you face down the hill, is the **Sicilian Garden**.
Open: April to September 09.00–17.00hrs; October, February and March 09.00–16.00hrs; November to January 09.00–15.00hrs.
Closed: 12.30–13.00hrs and first and third Monday in each month.

Chinese teahouse at Sanssouci

PEACE AND QUIET

Wildlife and Countryside in and around Berlin
by Paul Sterry

Although it is an unlikely seeming destination for anyone seeking relaxation or with an interest in natural history, in fact Berlin has much to offer within the city limits, and wildlife abounds further afield. Within Berlin itself there are numerous parks and gardens where you can relax and enjoy casual birdwatching, while the Grunewald Forest is a more extensive area of woodland within easy reach. By travelling further afield, superb areas of boggy heathland and forest can be found. Many of these have escaped the worst ravages of the modern world, unlike similar habitats elsewhere in western Europe.

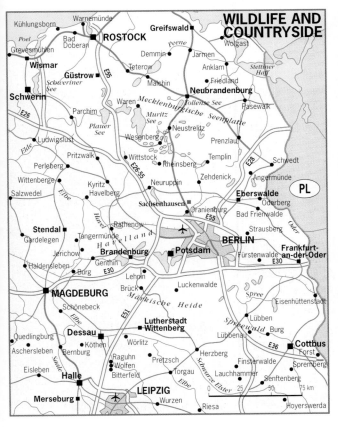

WILDLIFE AND COUNTRYSIDE

PEACE AND QUIET

The Tiergarten

The Tiergarten is an area of parkland containing the Zoo (Zoologischer Garten), which is open daily from 09.00hrs until sunset. In addition to lakes, it has extensive woodland which, although natural in appearance, is almost entirely replanted, the original vegetation having been devastated in 1945 during the Battle of Berlin. The Tiergarten is a good place for leisurely strolls and a surprising number of birds can be seen within its boundaries. The nearest station is the Zoo Station; the whole area is bisected by Strasse des 17 Juni.

Grunewald Forest

The most convenient way to explore the forest is to take a bus to the station at Strandbad Wannsee. From here, visitors can explore the extensive woodland – the whole area covers 12.5 square miles (32 sq km) – and walk along the shores of the Havel Lakes. Much of the forest was cut down after the war for firewood but thanks to extensive replanting you would hardly know. Birds, mammals and insects can be found among the pines, oaks and birches and it is easy to

A dappled path in the Grunewald

find a secluded spot to sit and contemplate. The largest lake – Grunewaldsee – is beloved of swimmers but also attracts waterbirds such as grebes and ducks out of season. There are several smaller lakes within the forest boundaries.

Volkspark Friedrichschain
Near the junction of Friedenstrasse and Am Friedrichschain in what was formerly East Berlin, Volkspark Friedrichschain is an extensive park, good for relaxing strolls. The wildlife interest is mainly limited to the human kind.

Weissensee
This lake and associated parkland area are northeast of Prenzlauer Berg, a suburb northeast of the centre of Berlin. It is a good place for strolling, with the chance of seeing wildfowl on the water.

Parks, Gardens and Lakes
In terms of wildlife, many of the smaller and more manicured parks and gardens will harbour little more than house sparrows, pigeons and starlings. However, some of the more extensive and overgrown areas attract a wider variety and offer more to visitors with an interest in natural history. In urban areas, woodland birds often become accustomed to the presence of man. Look for nuthatches and treecreepers feeding on trunks and branches. Both species have powerful feet that enable them to cling to vertical surfaces. Nuthatches are recognised by their dumpy appearance and blue-grey and tan plumage.

Thrush Nightingale
In the spring, large numbers of migrant birds arrive in the woodlands around Berlin to nest. Many of them, especially the warblers, have beautiful and distinctive songs with which they advertise their territories. However, perhaps the most attractive song – and certainly the loudest – belongs to a rather uniform brown bird known as a thrush nightingale or sprosser. Closely related to the nightingale of southern and western Europe, the smallish thrush nightingale has an even louder song than its relative. It comprises a mixture of loud 'chok' notes and a series of high-pitched and drawn-out calls repeated over and over again.

Treecreepers, on the other hand, have a streaked brown plumage and a thin, down-curved bill.

Among the smaller birds, look for robins, great tits, coal tits, chaffinches and woodpeckers. During migration times (April and May, then September and October) a wide range of other species, including warblers and flycatchers, pass through on their way to and from their breeding territories in northern Europe and their wintering grounds in southern Europe and Africa.

On lakes and ponds in Berlin, look for birds such as mallards, tufted ducks, pochards, coots and black-headed gulls. In the autumn and winter, several other species of wildfowl may appear, including goldeneyes, teal and shoveler.

PEACE AND QUIET

Although mammals have largely disappeared from the centre of Berlin, red squirrels can sometimes be seen in more remote areas of woodland around the outskirts of the city. They have orange-red fur, a tufted tail and tufted tips to the ears.

Further Afield

Compared to many parts of Europe, much of what formerly comprised East Germany is comparatively unspoilt. It is a land of heathland and boggy marsh, of forest and lake.

White-tailed eagle

Here, some of Europe's more threatened plants and animals survive and many are more abundant than anywhere else in Europe. Although almost any lake or area of forest or marsh that looks unspoilt is likely to harbour interesting wildlife, the following are some of the more important sites within reach of Berlin.

Schweriner See and Krakower See

These two lakes lie east of Schwerin, reached by driving northwest from Berlin on the E15 to Ludwigslust and then heading north to Schwerin. The waters of the lakes are nutrient rich and extremely productive, and harbour large numbers of fish and frogs. Reed-beds and alder carr woodlands fringe the margins, and gulls and terns breed on some of the protected islands. Ducks and geese pass through on migration and some stay the winter. Ospreys feed on

White-tailed Eagle

With a wingspan of about eight feet (250cm), the white-tailed eagle is the largest bird of prey to be seen in Germany. Adults are unmistakable in flight: with their broad wings they resemble a huge door in flight, and the white, wedge-shaped tail is characteristic. Juveniles, however, have brown tails and their shape must be used to identify them. White-tailed eagles breed around lakes and marshes and build large stick nests in trees. They feed on birds such as ducks as well as fish and carrion.

the fish in the lakes, while white-tailed eagles thrive on both the fish and the birds of the region.

Neubrandenburg and Neustrelitz

These two towns are north of Berlin and can be reached by driving on the E96 from the city. To the west of the road between the two towns are a series of lakes surrounded in places by marsh and woodland; explore this area using minor roads. The landscape shows much evidence of glaciation: the country is smooth and rolling, the lakes are shallow and the glacial moraines have woods of birch, alder, pine and oak. Sites which are particularly noteworthy include Galenbecker See, Tollense See and Kleines Haff, near Neubrandenburg, and Serrahn, to the east of Neustrelitz. On your way back to Berlin it is worth detouring to Wesenberg, southwest of Neustrelitz, and taking the minor road south to Rheinsberg. Interesting bog plants can be seen in all these areas, and grey herons, white-tailed eagles, lesser spotted eagles and cranes breed.

Brandenburg

Brandenburg lies on the flat Havel Plain west of Berlin. It is a region of lakes and marshes and the haunt of wetland birds and flowers. Several lakes can be found around the perimeter of Brandenburg itself. One of the most interesting is the Reitzer See, to the southeast. The lake itself is the haunt of wildfowl while the surrounding marsh has an interesting flora.

Common crane spying out the land

Urwald Breitefenn

This area of virgin forest lies northeast of Berlin between Oderberg and Parstein. To reach it, head out of the city on the road to Bad Freienwalde. Pass through the town and before you reach Altglietzen turn left to Oderberg and on to Parstein. In addition to forest, there is marsh and open water here. At Plagefenn, northeast of Eberswalde, is a reserve where wet woodland and open water (Plagesee) can be found.

Schlaubetal

To reach this valley drive east from Berlin on the E8 to Frankfurt-an-der-Oder and then south to Eisenhüttenstadt. Here, visitors will find heathland, lakes and forest and a wealth of bird and plant life.

PEACE AND QUIET

Lübben

Near Lubben can be found the Lower Spree Forest (Spreewald), on the edge of which is a nature reserve at Kriegbusch. The River Spree ensures a rich growth of marsh plants in the alder carr woodland, with oaks and hornbeams growing on drier ground. Storks nest in the trees here.

Untere Mulde

The River Mulde between Dessau and Bitterfeld is a good area to look for beavers. Drive south from Berlin on the E6 and, in the vicinity of Dessau take the minor road to Raguhn which runs parallel to the river on its east side. Part of the area is a nature reserve set up to protect the forest and beavers.

A long-leaved sundew taking lunch

Bogs and Heathland

Heathland is a type of habitat that is found on sandy soils which are acidic in nature, low in nutrients and often well drained. To the south and east of Berlin, tracts of heathland still persist and species of heathers are typical plants of this terrain. Where valley bottoms are found, water collects and bogs form; these habitats are rich in interesting plant life. Sundews – plants with sticky leaves – supplement their diet by catching and digesting insects, and there are often large tracts of cottongrass, bog myrtle and *Sphagnum* moss studded with heath spotted orchids in summer. Waders and ducks breed in the bogs and, where patches of woodland form, birds such as bluethroats and hen harriers can be found.

Forest birds

Forests and woodlands around Berlin harbour a wide variety of birds including some which are quite difficult to see in western Europe. Golden orioles are often common summer visitors. Although the males are bright yellow in colour – females are duller – they are hard to see among dappled foliage. However, their loud, fluty song carries a considerable distance and is quite unmistakable. Many birds of prey also breed in the region. Red kites and black kites – both recognised by their forked tails – are often common, and lesser spotted eagles are sometimes seen. Although juveniles have white spots, adults are a rather uniform brown colour. In flight, they have broad wings and a short, wedge-shaped tail.

FOOD AND DRINK

Traditional German cuisine is not in the top ranks of European gastronomy, but what it lacks in subtlety, it makes up for in quantity.

The *Berliner Schlachteplatte* consists of boiled pork, liver sausage and pigs' kidneys with potatoes and *sauerkraut* (pickled cabbage). *The* Berlin meat dish is *Eisbein*, knuckle of pork with *sauerkraut* and *Erbspüree* (mashed peas). Near forest areas, you might find *Wildschweinbraten* – roast wild boar; *Schlesisches Himmelreich* means either roast pork or goose with potato dumplings in gravy; *Spanferkel* is suckling pig; and *Königsbergerklopse* means meatballs in cream. Potatoes are served up as *Kartoffelpuffer* (fried potato cakes), *Kartoffelsuppe* (potato soup with chunks of bacon and a parsley garnish) and *Pellkartoffeln mit Quark* (jacket potatoes with curd cheese, plus optional linseed oil). Fish figures large in local cuisine, with pickled herring, the more delicate *Matjeshering* (raw herring fillets with apple, onion and gherkins in cream) and *Aal grün* – eels in herb sauce, possibly caught in the nearby River Havel. There are numerous types of traditional bread.

All this has been displaced in many restaurants by the 'new German cuisine', which emphasises fresh products, imaginative recipes and smaller portions; and the range of other national cuisines is large. There are any number of Italian restaurants, and Turkish food is popular as well, both as served in *Schnellimbiss* (fast food) bars on every street corner, and in reasonably priced restaurants. There is also a choice of Chinese, Thai, Egyptian, Spanish, French, Japanese and American (both north and south) cuisines.

Where to Eat

In a city that stays up all night, there is always somewhere to get a decent meal. Possibilities range from the *Kneipe* (corner pub and snack bar), to cafés (some open all day and most of the night for drinks and meals),

Coffee at Kranzler on the Ku'damm

FOOD AND DRINK

as well as rather more formal restaurants. In between meals, there is always the *Konditorei* (cake and coffee shop). Most famous of these is the **Kranzler**, one of the cafés where intellectuals met from the early years of the 19th century. Formerly in the Friedrichstrasse in the East, the Kranzler was transferred after World War II to the Kurfürstendamm in the West.

Every *Rathaus*, or town hall, has a café in the basement, called the *Ratskeller*. This is usually a large civic establishment serving good food at a reasonable price.

Mealtimes

Breakfast in Berlin is a day-long event, served in some cafés from 08.30hrs until midnight. German breakfast is normally a selection of cold meats, pâté and cheese with a variety of bread. Most Berliners have both lunch (the main meal of the day) and their evening meal relatively early – from 12.00 and 18.00hrs respectively.

Drink

Berlin is predominantly a beer city with a couple of well-known local breweries – Berliner Kindl and Schultheiss (the latter now part of a larger national brewery). Locally brewed East German beers, once esteemed by experts, are now in shorter supply given the craze for all things Western. If you want draught beer, ask for 'Bier vom Fass'. A popular summer drink is the *Berliner Weisse mit Schuss*, a low-alcohol beer flavoured with a shot of pink raspberry

juice or extract of green woodruff.

Germany also produces a wide range of hock-type white wines, some of them fruity. Red wines, all from the southwest, are very few.

Restaurants

The old West of the city has always been known as a temple to consumerism so the visitor will not be surprised to find the busiest restaurants and the most feverish nightlife here. The district around Europa Center and the Ku'damm is full of bars and restaurants patronised by tourists. You are likely to find more local life as you range further afield to, say, the area around Savignyplatz, Wilmersdorfer Strasse or Kreuzberg. Mitte and the old East of the city still lag behind but, judging by the development around Freidrichstrasse and Unter den Linden, not for long. For the moment, the biggest concentration of restaurants remains in the Nikolaiviertel, patronised mostly by tourists. For all the more formal restaurants, booking is advisable.

West Central Area

Arche Noah, Fasenenstrasse 79 (tel: 88 26 138). A kosher restaurant on the first floor of the Jüdisches Gemeindehaus serves Middle Eastern specialities. On Thursday evenings, a hot and cold buffet with a choice of 30 dishes.
Bamberger Reiter, Regensburgerstrasse 7 (tel: 21 84 282). Excellent French

cuisine won this establishment a Michelin star. The bistro next door belongs to the same management.

Bovril, Kufürstendamm 184 (tel: 881 8461). Smart bistro with good set meals as well as a varied à la carte menu. Eat outside in the summer.

Café Hardenberg, Hardenbergstrasse (tel: 312 3330). This is a young person's café, full of undergraduates in serious discussion and even more serious beer drinking. Bicycle park outside; loud music.

Carpe Diem, Savigny Passage 577 (tel: 313 2728). Tapas and Mediterranean seafood are served under the railway arches of the S-Bahn. Attracts a young crowd.

Court Carrée, Savignyplatz 5 (tel: 312 5238). Located on a broad corner of the Savignyplatz, with views of the lively square. Good French food, garden seating in summer.

Dicke Wirtin, Carmerstrasse 9 (tel: 312 4952). Popular dark brown Berlin pub, with walls covered in posters and paintings and mirrors. Serves cheap and filling soups.

Einhorn, Wittenbergerplatz 5–6 (tel: 218 6347). In a city where vegetarians have not made much of a mark, this cheap and cheerful wholefood shop and vegetarian restaurant is a bonus. There's another branch at Mommsenstrasse 2.

Einstein, Kurfürstenstrasse 58 (tel: 261 5096). A large old-fashioned café on the ground floor of a neo-classical house which once belonged to Henny Porten, star of silent films. Young

Berliner Weisse beers. Beer is the staple alcoholic drink

FOOD AND DRINK

There are plenty of informal eating places in the centre

waiters in tails serve an artistic and literary set. Gardens to the rear.

Hardtke, Meinekestrasse 27 (tel: 881 9827). This old-fashioned Berlin-style restaurant – dark wood panelling, old oil lamps hanging over wooden tables, and waiters in waistcoats and aprons – serves traditional Berliner food at reasonable prices. There's another branch at Hubertusallee 48, Wilmersdorf.

Jimmy's Diner, Pariser Strasse 41 (tel: 882 3141). '50s diner with abundant plastic and chrome and serving good Tex-Mex food. Alternatively, Route 66 is another '50s diner on the corner of Esmar and Pariser Strasse.

Lutter & Wegner, Schlüterstrasse 55 (tel: 881 3440). Formerly – from 1811 – a wine bar in the east of the city, opened as a restaurant here after World War II. Old fashioned décor but nouvelle cuisine and an emphasis on fine wine.

Schwarzes Café, Kantstrasse 148 (tel: 313 8038). A 24-hour bar which only closes during the day on Tuesday. Plenty of atmosphere and good food.

Shell, Knesebeckstrasse 22 (tel: 312 8310). White tablecloths, bentwood chairs, and plain wooden floors – the décor is simple, but this restaurant is lively, cheerful and always busy.

Wintergarten, Fasanenstrasse 23 (tel: 882 5414). The house is a meeting place for anybody involved in books, with a bookshop in the basement and a café extension – open to all. Excellent food, good value.

Zlata Praha, Meinekestrasse 4 (tel: 881 9750). A comfortable *fin de siècle* atmosphere in this Czech restaurant which also serves a variety of Hungarian dishes. Liberal use of cream and paprika.

Around Kreuzberg

Altes Zollhaus, Carl-Herz-Ufer 30 (tel: 692 3300). Former customs house on the Landwehrkanal is now a restaurant with a considerable reputation in Berlin. Pricey but popular.

Café Addis, Templhofer-Ufer 6 (tel: 251 6730). Ethiopian food – spicy meat stews and *njera* bread (like large thin pancakes). Cutlery is provided but those who know how, eat with their hands.

Die Rote Harfe, Oranienstrasse 13. Cheap German beer,

Guinness or steaming cups of cappuccino and cheerful company. Despite a hot political reputation, it is the sort of place you can bring a baby in a pushchair. Food upstairs. Similar establishments at the **Elefanta** next door.

Max und Moritz, Oranienstrasse 162, Sober and traditional. Unusually for Berlin, it asks anybody not actually eating to sit at the bar rather than an empty table. Blackboard menu.

Noodle Company, Yorckstrasse 84 (tel: 785 2736). Pasta and noodles in all styles, European and Oriental.

Mitte, Nikolaiviertel and Prenzlauer Berg

Berliner Ratskeller, Rotes Rathaus, Rathausstrasse. The civic café/restaurant of the Red Town Hall is divided into a beer restaurant at one end and a wine restaurant (more expensive) at the other. Dancing on Wednesdays, Thursdays and Sundays after 19.00hrs.

Café Oren, Oranienburger Strasse 28 (tel: 282 8228). Next to the New Synagogue, this is a Jewish but not kosher restaurant. Attractive surroundings and good food with a Middle Eastern flavour.

Französicher Hof, Jägerstrasse 36 (tel: 229 3152). In a lovely position on the splendid Gendarmenmarkt, this restaurant serves classic French and German dishes.

Mark Brandenburg Restaurant, Mohrenstrasse 30 (tel: 23 820). Restaurant of the Hilton Hotel specialises in local dishes like braised ox with root vegetables – in a comfortable setting.

FOOD AND DRINK/SHOPPING

Offenbach-Stuben,
Stubbenkammerstrasse 8 (tel:
445 8502). Long-established
family restaurant in Prenzlauer
Berg. Serves German food,
Berlin specialties. The 'rustical
plate' is not for slimmers.
Operncafé, Unter den Linden 5
(tel: 200 0256). Coffee and
cakes to one side, smart bar to
the other and restaurant
upstairs. This most elegant of
Berlin's cafés has terrace
seating in the summer.
Pasternak, Knaackstrasse 22–4
(tel: 441 3391). Cheerful and
always crowded, this
bar/restaurant serves Russian
food. **Tantalus**, **Anita Wronski**
and **Gaststätte am Wasserturm**,
adjoining retaurants, are also
cheerful and crowded.
Restaurant Ephraim Palais,
Poststrasse 16 (tel: 217 13164).
In a splendid location adjoining
the palace and backing on to the
Spree canal. Discreet plush and
comfort inside.
Restauration 1900, corner of
Husemannstrasse and
Wörtherstrasse. A classy
restaurant, supposedly
patronised by artists.
Zum Nussbaum,
Propstrasse/Am Nussbaum (tel:
2171 3328). An old Berlin pub,
modelled on one frequented by
the local, much-loved cartoonist,
Heinrich Zille (1858–1929). The
whole of this steeply gabled
house in front of Nikolaikirche
has been entirely restored.
Zum Paddenwirt,
Nikolaikircheplatz 6 (tel: 2171
3231). Just behind the
Nikolaikirche, a comfortable
old-style bar and eatery with
good German home cooking.
Also restored.

SHOPPING

At present the visitor will find the
best shopping in the west
central district of the city. But
things are changing fast. Judging
by the galleries of smart shops
already in the Nikolaiviertel and
those planned for
Freidrichstrasse, Unter den
Linden and Alexanderplatz,
Mitte may soon be a shopping
mecca too. Galeries Lafayette is
moving into the new
Friedrichstradt Passagen
arcade. At present, in the old
East, Nikolaiviertel is the place
for posh shopping and the large
supermarket, Kaufhaus, on
Alexanderplatz, for run-of-the-
mill goods.

Basics
There are excellent shopping
areas, patronised by locals, in
the main streets of all the
various boroughs and districts.
Examples are: Karl-Marx-
Strasse in Neukölln with cheap
boutiques where you might find
leather goods, particularly at the
Hermannplatz U-Bahn end;
Wilmersdorfer Strasse in
Charlottenburg, for a range of
shops and department stores;
Schlossstrasse, near the U-Bahn
in Steglitz; and the
pedestrianised Old Town in
Spandau. In addition, there is
the Europa-Center, a glitzy
rather than glamorous building
of shops and offices just by the
Breitscheidplatz, with a variety
of middle-range goods for sale.

Upmarket
The most expensive shops are
to be found in the Ku'damm,
near the Breitscheidplatz end,

and in the smaller streets running off this thoroughfare. No visitor should come to Berlin without entering the portals of its most famous shop – the Ka De We, short for Kaufhaus des Westens, a department store established since the 1880s in Wittenbergplatz. The sixth floor is entirely given over to food and drink, both to take home and for immediate consumption (pick your own fresh fish, to be grilled while you wait, toying with a glass of *Sekt*, Germany's champagne equivalent). Locals vote the sales staff the most helpful and knowledgeable of any. The Wertheim department store, run by the same company as Ka De We, offers a smaller range of goods at lower prices, at Kurfürstendamm 231. Hertie, Karstadt and Quelle are three good department stores, all on Wilmersdorfe Strasse. Immediately you turn off the Ku'damm into Fasanenstrasse, the atmosphere is altogether more refined. Valentino

Busking at the Europa-Center

SHOPPING

Garavani at no 74 sells small and expensive gifts. This is the place to buy that special souvenir of Berlin – a solid gold bear. Past the pink brick façade of the Literaturhaus and the Käthe Kollwitz Museum, you can peep into some of the most prestigious art galleries in Berlin. The Galerie Nagel (no 42) is a photographer's gallery, the Antiquitäten Kabinett at no 73 sells fine antique jewellery. Christie's auction house is here at no 72 and Cartier at no 28. Patrick Hellmann sells his fashion clothes from no 26, just one of his five shops. On Pariser Strasse, Galerie Janssen is a homoerotic gallery and bookshop, Champ sells excellent men's clothes in German style, and you can buy anything sporty from Citysport.

Cross into Bleibtreustrasse and at no 27 Hosta Rennert sells designer clothes with a pazazz that has you almost reaching into your wallet. At no 29 opposite, Bleibgrün has a selection of perfectly extraordinary shoes. You'll find more shoes, including styles by Salvatore Ferragamo, at Budapester Shoes (reputedly the best men's shoe shop in Berlin). Beautiful hand-made ceramics are on sale at Knesebeckstrasse 32 and hand-crafted jewellery by Lisa Lotila-Puchert at Mommemstrasse 3.

Secondhand and Vintage Clothes

The Garage, a huge basement warehouse in Ahornstrasse, Nollendorf, sells racks of shirts, jeans, coats, hats and shoes by the kilo. The best place for period clothes is Spitze, at Weimarer Strasse 19, which stocks clothes from 1860 to 1960. Otherwise there's Falbala at Ludwigkirchstrasse 9a.

Markets

The Antik-und Flohmarkt is an indoor flea market under the S-Bahn tracks at Friedrichstrasse station with about 100 stalls. The weekend market at Strasse des 17 Juni, near the Tiergarten S-Bahn, sells top quality goods at one end (good antiques, china, glass) and crafts and knick-knacks at the other. Kreuzberg has the Sunday Krempelmarkt at Reichpietschufer, and Wilmersdorf holds a Sunday secondhand market at Fehrbelliner Platz.

There is an open air food market in every district, often in the square outside the *Rathaus* (town hall).

For colour and spectacle, go to the Turkish market held at Maybachufer in Neukölln, on Tuesday and Friday 12.00–18.00hrs. Here you will find olives, cheeses, live chickens and rabbits, and always the scent of spices.

Specialities

Speciality shops tend to be grouped in certain areas. For German antique furniture try the shops in Keithstrasse and Eisenacher Strasse in Schöneberg. For books, the area near the Technische Universität, around Knesebeckstrasse and Hardenbergstrasse, has shops which stock German and foreign language books in

The Sunday market, Strasse des 17 Juni

specialist subjects. For a large stock of books in English, try The British Bookshop at Mauerstrasse 83–4 in Mitte. For new fashion, jewellery and furniture design, keep an eye on the art and craft shops in the Schöneberg/Kreuzberg area. The Berliner Zinnfiguren (Berlin Tin Soldier), Knesebeckstrasse 88, is an old-established shop with over 30,000 model soldiers for sale, ready moulded or for home moulding. Fine porcelain is sold in all the better shops. The showrooms of the Königliche Porzellanmanufaktur (Royal Porcelain Factory) are on Wegelystrasse by the Tiergarten S-Bahn.

For souvenirs of Berlin, the shops attached to museums always have some small and interesting items. The plaster-casting shop of the State Museum at Sophie-Charlotten-Strasse 17–18 sells copies of notable busts and statues at a reasonable price.

ACCOMMODATION

There is a wide choice of accommodation in Berlin, ranging from expensive, luxury hotels to cheap pensions and *Privat Unterkunft* (bed and breakfast). There is a nucleus around Zoo Station and the Ku'damm, but the excellent public transport network makes a hotel outside the centre possible. Mitte has always had quality hotels, and more are being built all the time. However, the visitor who chooses an inexpensive stay in the former East, particularly outside the centre, should not yet expect the standards considered normal in central Berlin.

It is now possible to book a hotel in any part of Berlin directly, or, if you prefer, via the tourist office in Berlin, at least two weeks before your trip, at Verkehrsamt Berlin, Europa-Center, 1000 Berlin 30 (tel: 262 6031). Explain how long you want to stay and the type and price of accommodation you are after. A small fee is charged. For longer stays, the Mitwohnzentrale apartment sharing centre can arrange accommodation in a variety of private properties: the address is 3rd floor, Ku'damm Eck, Kurfürstendamm 227–8, Berlin (tel: (030) 882 6694).

Expensive
West Central
Bristol Hotel Kempinski, Kurfürstendamm 27, Berlin 10719 (tel: 884 34-0). This modern hotel evokes an earlier splendour. Classy and luxurious, favoured by knowledgeable transatlantic visitors.
Inter-Continental Berlin, Budapesterstrasse 2, Berlin

The plush Hotel Inter-Continental

10787 (tel: 26020). Berlin's biggest hotel, with 600 rooms. Near the Europa-Center and Tiergarten, with all the usual facilities of a very expensive hotel.

Steigenberger Berlin, Los Angeles Platz 1, Berlin 10789 (tel: 21 080). Large and efficient, central but quietly situated.

Mitte

Berlin Hilton, Mohrenstrasse 30, Berlin 10117 (tel: 2382). New, luxury, central hotels with eight restaurants. Light and spacious with greenery and running water. There are special rooms for non-smokers and guests with disabilities.

Maritim Grand Hotel, Friedrichstrasse 158–64, Berlin 10117 (tel: 23270). Arguably the best hotel in all Berlin. Hotel restaurant on the first floor; separate luxury restaurant on the seventh; shopping arcade and fitness club.

Radisson Plaza Hotel, Karl-Liebknecht Strasse 5, Berlin 10178 (tel: 2410). Ideal position facing Museumsinsel and the cathedral, newly renovated and extremely comfortable.

Potsdam

Schloss Cecilienhof, Neuer Garten, Potsdam (tel: 23141-41). This comfortable hotel is part of the Cecilienhof which hosted the Potsdam Conference in 1945, and is surrounded by attractive grounds. Out of town – you would need your own transport.

Medium

West Central

Art Hotel Sorat, Joachimstaler Strasse 28–9, Berlin 10719 (tel: 88 4470). Public areas and bedrooms are decorated with paintings and sculptures. This hotel (at the very top of the medium price range) is for design-conscious aesthetes. .

Berlin Plaza Hotel, Knesebeckstrasse 63, Berlin 10719 (tel: 884 130). 3-star hotel just off Kufürstendamm. Modern, comfortable and friendly. Parking facilities.

Charlot, Giesebrechstrasse 17, Berlin 10629 (tel: 323 4051). An excellent value hotel for its central position near the Adenauerplatz U-bahn stop.

Meineke, Meinekestrasse 10, Berlin 10719 (tel: 228 8111). Old fashioned, not luxurious, not expensive, but comfortable and near the Ku'damm.

Mitte

Gendarm Garni Hotel, Charlottenstrasse 60, Berlin 10117 (tel: 200 4180). On two floors of an old town house. Very central, friendly and immaculately decorated.

Hotel Luisenhof, Köpenicker Strasse 92, Berlin 10179 (tel: 270 0543). Newly converted 1820s house. Elegant and convenient.

Cheap

Lower-priced hotels and pensions may not have a bath or shower in every room.

West Central

Bogota, Schlüterstrasse 45, Berlin 10707 (tel: 881 5001). A reasonably priced, central hotel. Comfortable rooms and friendly atmosphere.

Econtel Berlin, Sömmeringstrasse 24, Berlin 105889 (tel: 34 6810). Near the

ACCOMMODATION

Luxurious Bristol Hotel Kempinski

Schloss Charlottenburg. Cots, bottle-warming facilities, and discounts for children sharing their parents' room; easy public transport to centre.

Hotelpension Dittberner, Wielanstrasse 25, Berlin 10707 (tel: 88 46 950). On the upper floor of a building that also houses an art gallery.

Hotel-Pension Elba, Bleibtreustrasse 26, Berlin 10707 (tel: 881 7504). This hotel, a substantial town house in a central location, is clean, comfortable and good value.

Hotel-Pension Wittelsbach, Wittlesbacherstrasse 22, Berlin 10707 (tel: 861 4371). Near U-Bahn Konstanze Strasse. A family hotel, geared to children, with a playroom indoors and a garden play area.

Pension München, Güntselstrasse 62, Berlin 31 (tel: 857 9120). Small, upper-floor pension, three stops on U-Bahn from Zoo Station.

Pension Niebuhr, Niebuhrstrasse 74, Berlin 10629 (tel: 324 9595). Situated in a quiet area but close to Ku'damm; welcomes children.

Pension Silvia, Knesebeckstrasse 29, Berlin 10623 (tel: 881 2129). Well run by the redoubtable Silvia.

Mitte

Hotel Fischerinsel, Neue Rosstrasse 11, Berlin 10179 (tel: 23 80 7700). Not luxurious but everything functions, the service is friendly and location central.

Hotel Merkur, Torstrasse 156, Berlin 10115 (tel: 282 8297). A simple but clean hotel just north of Oranienburg Strasse.

CULTURE, ENTERTAINMENT AND NIGHTLIFE

As well as regular festivals, including the Berlin Film Festival, the city offers some of the best classical music, opera and theatre in the world. There also exists a range of activity in experimental theatre, experimental dance, jazz, rock, pop and international music, together with circus arts and puppetry. Since reunification, the uncertainty of continued funding has slowed some of this down.

There are also light plays and comedies on offer in the commercial theatre, as well as the discos, casinos and nightclubs. Here, the Berlin predilection is for 'travestie' or drag shows – once considered the height of sophistication, though the audiences these days are mostly middle-aged men from the provinces. ,

Berlin has two good listings magazines – *Zitty* and *Tip*. The Tourist Office publishes a monthly *Berlin Programme,* and there is an independent English-language listings magazine – *Metropolis.*

For the most popular shows, it is almost impossible to get tickets at short notice from regular box offices. Use the ticket agencies or Theaterkassen, at the Europa-Center, Tauentzienstrasse 9 (tel: 261 70 51/52), Ka De We department store, Tauentzienstrasse 21 (tel: 248 036), and Wertheim, Kurfürstendamm 231 (tel: 882 2500).

Hans Scharoun's brilliantly designed Philharmonie concert hall, home of the Berlin Philharmonic Orchestra

CULTURE, ENTERTAINMENT AND NIGHTLIFE

Classical style: Deutsche Staatsoper

Classical Music

Classical music at Tiergarten is dominated by the Berlin Philharmonic under conductor Claudio Abbado. Their home is the dramatic **Philharmonie** building in the Tiergarten – designed by Hans Scharoun and worth a look in its own right. The seats go right around the concert hall, in a plan inspired by the way people gather naturally around the source of music.

Tickets for major concerts are difficult to obtain, but there are always smaller concerts or recitals. The **Deutsche Oper**, Bismarckstrasse 34, offers a classical music programme as well as opera and ballet. The city is also full of small orchestras and music groups performing regularly at a variety of venues.

The main concert hall in Mitte is the **Konzerthaus** in Gendarmenmarkt. The Berliner Sinfonie Orchester and the Deutches Sinfonie-Orchester, whose chief conductor is Vladimir Ashkenazy, are the star attractions. But within a stone's throw there is also the Deutche Staatsoper as well as the Komische Oper, so the choice is great. Tickets are no longer as cheap as they used to be.

Jazz, Rock and Folk

Deutschlandhalle, **Eissporthalle** and the **ICC Berlin** are the largest of Berlin's many conference venues which are also used for music. The **Haus der Kulturen der Welt** in the Tiergarten serves the same dual function.

The **Waldbühne**, the huge amphitheatre near the Olympic Stadium, attracts world-famous artists. The **'Tempodrom'** is two tents set up in the Tiergarten to house a variety of entertainment, including live music in the summer.

Jazz enthusiasts are well catered for at the **A-Trane**, Bleibtreustrasse 1 in Charlottenburg. Also in Charlottenburg **Ewige Lampe** at Neibuhrstrasse 11a features international bands. For traditional jazz music, **Eierschale** at Rankestrasse 1, near the Gedächtniskirche, is a popular venue. **Quasimodo**, Kantstrasse 12a and **Blues Café**, Körnerstrasse 11 also have their aficionados. Middling-famous rock bands perform at the **Metropol**, Nollendorf Platz 5. The **Loft**, part of the Metropol, hosts smaller bands with a more experimental flavour.

Under the spotlight at the Big Eden disco on Kufürstendamm

East of Brandenburg Gate

Large concert venues like the **Radrennbahn** in Weissensee have often hosted bands and performers well known in the West. **Parkhaus**, Puschkinallee 5 at Treptow hosted jazz bands throughout the Socialist era. At Mitte, **Podewil**, Klosterstrasse 68–70 has a wide-ranging musical programme with a strong jazz element.

Clubs and Discos

Discos in the west of the city are thick on the ground with a rapid turnover of name and style. Few operate an entrance charge. This is a small selection: **Abraxas**, Kantstrasse 134, has free entry and the rhythm is mostly Latin. At **Blue Note**, Courbierestrasse 13, there is a small charge on Friday and Saturday night, with Latin and jazz a speciality. **Dschungel**, Nürnbergerstrasse 53, has been voted one of the best by those in the know, with **Cha-Cha,** next door at Nürnbergerstrasse 50,

CULTURE, ENTERTAINMENT AND NIGHTLIFE

second. **Big Eden** and **Far Out,** both on Kufürstendamm, cater for night-time ravers.

The liveliest night-spots east of Brandenburg Gate are probably in the Prenzlauer Berg and Mitte areas. The best way to negotiate the changing scene is by word of mouth. If your German is not up to it, keep an eye on the listings magazines but do not expect much activity before midnight. **E-Werk**, **Electro** and **Kitchen**, all in Mitte, are for Techno-ravers. The **Yucca Bar**, in Pankow at Neumannstrasse 136, **Café Lolott** and **Café Nord**, both on Schönhauser Allee, **Ballhaus Berlin**, Chausseestrasse 108, in Mitte, with table telephones, and in Mitte, **Clärchens Ballhaus**, Auguststrasse 24–5 are strictly for the middle-aged.

Cabaret and Revue

The most extravagant variety revue show is in Mitte, in the **Friedrichstadtpalast** (tel: 283 6474). Here, celebrity performers share the programme with dancing girls and variety acts. The Kleine Revue – the Small Revue – in the same building, is more intimate and adult. After the show ends at midnight, the stage becomes a dance floor. The **Europa-Center** is the home of La Vie En Rose revue; a lot of dancing girls in feathers and pearls and not much else. Also in the Europa-Center is the political cabaret, Die Stachelschweine – the Hedgehogs – considered not nearly sharp enough by some. **Chez Nous**, at Marburger Strasse 14, Tiergarten, has a dragshow that might remind

visitors of Berlin's saucy reputation in the 30s but is relatively innocent. The **BKA** (Berlin Kabaret Anstalt) performs at Mehringdamm 34 in Kreuzberg, but, as with all cabaret shows, you need a decent command of the language to fully appreciate the performance. This is not essential at the **Wintergarten-Variete**, at Potsdamerstrasse 96, where there is enough singing and dancing to entertain.

Dance

There is a strong tradition of experimental and modern dance in the city. It was in Berlin that Isadora Duncan opened her first school. The **Tanzfabrik**, Mockernstrasse 68, in Kreuzberg, was formed as a collective to practise and teach dance theatre and experimental dance forms, and has a considerable reputation. The **Tanz Tangente** company on Kuhligshofstrasse 4 also performs and teaches. The State ballet school, **Staatliche Balletschule Berlin**, has about 200 students at its premises in Prenzlauer Berg.

Theatre

The great Berlin theatrical tradition has always been concentrated in what became the city's East sector. The **Berliner Ensemble**, at Bertolt-Brecht-Platz 1, is still the official Bertolt Brecht Theatre, with a large repertoire of his work. There has been controversy lately, however, and the theatre has been criticised for fossilisation. The **Volksbühne**, Rosa Luxemburg-Platz, and the

CULTURE, ENTERTAINMENT AND NIGHTLIFE

Deutsches Theater (where Max Reinhardt was a director), at Schumannstrasse 13a–14, are other notable venues in the former East.

Opera and ballet performances take place in the **Deutsche Oper**, Bismarckstrasse 35, and also at the **Komische Oper**, Behrenstrasse 55–7, and the **Staatsoper**, Unter den Linden 7, both in Mitte.

The **Hebbel Theater**, at Stresemannstrasse 29 in Kreuzberg, is probably Berlin's most prestigious theatre company outside the large state-run companies. The resident director is Peter Stein. For musicals and comedies try **Komödie** and the **Theater am Kufürstendamm**, both of which are at Kufürstendamm 206. The **Theater des Westens**, Kantstrasse 12, and **Hansa-**

Deutsches Theater, a national stage

Theater, Alt-Moabit 47, usually have a light-hearted repertoire. The **UFA-Fabrik** at Viktoriastrasse 13 is a cultural 'factory' in Kreuzberg. Alternative Berliners swear by this venue for theatre, dance, music and film.

Film

The cinemas in the Ku'damm and around Breitscheidplatz show the latest international films. Most of them are dubbed unless they carry the letters OF (*Originalfassung* – original soundtrack) or OmU (*Originalfassung mit Untertiteln* – original soundtrack with German subtitles). The best time to see international movies is during the Berlin Film Festival in February.

WEATHER AND WHEN TO GO

Berlin has a continental climate, with cold, crisp winters and surprisingly hot summers. If you want to sample the *Berliner Luft* (Berlin air) in comfort, visit between April (maximum temperature in the low 70s Fahrenheit/low 20s Centigrade) and June (mid-80s Fahrenheit/upper 20s Centigrade).

The Botanischer Garten is one of many green spaces in Berlin

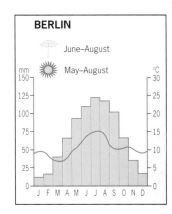

BERLIN

June–August

May–August

HOW TO BE A LOCAL

Berliners have a reputation for being more tolerant and relaxed than the citizens of other German cities. In the years leading up to unification, West Germans of a radical or alternative persuasion, young men wishing to avoid military service, gay people, political activists and intellectuals found a congenial home in West Berlin. The eastern sector of the city, as capital of East Germany, seemed stiff and starchy by comparison – though it was also home to artists and intellectuals. There are many Berlin people who are by no means raving bohemians, whichever side of the one-time Wall they come from. Indeed, some may appear reserved and conservative, surrounded by a private space which seems a little greater than the usual reticence of big-city dwellers.

In the months following unification, with the onset of capitalism and a release from rigid ideology, a small minority in the East began to use their new-found freedom somewhat aggressively. Racist attacks, vandalism and football hooliganism all increased. If promises of economic parity fail to materialise and disappointments continue, this phenomenon will not go away. This being said, Berlin is nine parts out of ten a safe and unconfrontational city, where a woman may walk unwhistled at and unmolested, free to dine alone in a restaurant without arousing comment. Mugging and personal violence is far less frequent than in London, say, or in modern Madrid. What strikes one most is how thoroughly peaceable the majority appear to be – partly, perhaps, in reaction to the shocking portions of their own history, partly because they know the horrors of war as thoroughly as any group in Europe. The abhorrence of violence, both in national and personal affairs, is matched by a love of nature, a passionate attachment to green and open places. This is common to most Germans, but is seems to be at its most intense in West Berlin in particular. People there are fiercely environmentalist. Their passion presumably derives from the fact that for almost 50 years they were boxed inside their city, which does however have many lakes and forests within its limits. The moment the sun shines, and even when it does not, Berliners flock to the woods and fan out along the cycle tracks. There are any number of outings and hikes. (See the information magazines *Zitty* and *Tip* or phone the Fahrverband Wandern, the hiking association, tel: 452 4576).

Berliners love water. But then, they are surrounded by it – the Havel and Spree rivers, interconnecting canals and the Wannsee, Müggelsee and Tegeler See lakes. The most popular and the most crowded bathing place on summer days is the Wannsee, said to be the largest inland beach in Europe. It is well served by restaurants, play areas and showers, and offers boats, pedaloes and hooded, wicker beach chairs for hire.

Local loyalty is very important in Berlin. People owe allegiance to their own borough – and claim you can tell the citizens of each by their own accents – but even more so their own tiny neighbourhood or patch of city streets, known in German as their *Kiez*.

Berliners love ice-cream and coffee and cake at all times of the day. Beer is a serious drink and the pouring of beer is an art form. Patience is the key. Expect to wait seven minutes from the time you order your drink before it arrives at your table. Berliner Weisse, beer spiked with raspberry or green woodruff syrup, is a summer speciality. Locals insist this coloured froth is only drunk by tourists – untrue. But it is probably true you lose all claim to be a serious beer drinker if you are caught sipping it through a straw.

All restaurant bills carry a 17 per cent service charge. If you give a tip, it should be handed to your waiter rather than left on the table.

In general, Berliners respect authority. Jaywalking is not only frowned on, it is also a fining offence. Drinking and driving is considered unacceptable. Family life is surprisingly formal. Children are not made much of, compared to those in more southerly countries. Seen and not heard appears to be the rule for public places. The time to visit family members – parents or in-laws – is for afternoon coffee on Sundays.

CHILDREN

Numerous puppet theatre groups aim their work at children, putting on shows which present no language problem for visitors. Berlin Figurentheater, Yorckstrasse 59, Fliegenotes Theatre, Gneisenaustrasse 2, and the UFA-Fabrik, Viktoriastrasse 13–18, usually have something that appeals to young people. The amount of open green space in the city is a bonus for children. The Tiergarten, Grunewald woods, Teufelsberg, lakes and canals all provide

some opportunity for swimming and watersports. The Ernst Thälmann Pionierpark is an amusement park in the Wühlheide woods in Köpenick. From Köpenick Altstadt, there are Weisse Flotte boat trips to the Grosser Müggelsee. The Zoo and its aquarium are old standbys. Children might also like to explore the Tierpark, a much larger zoo in the eastern suburb of Friedrichsfelde, where the animals roam freer in family groups.

Many of the exhibits in the Museum für Verkehr und Technik can be given the hands-on treatment

All the Berlin museums have something to offer children. The Museen Dahlem has a separate section which has been designed especially for children, and the Museum für Verkehr und Technik is a draw for anyone who likes computers or mechanical things. Checkpoint Charlie has most children transfixed.

TIGHT BUDGET

- Buy a 3-day Welcome Card which gives you unlimited travel throughout the city on all buses, trams, trains and BVG ferries, for 72 hours plus reductions on entry prices to major places of interest.
- A six-day ticket, the Sammelkarte, allows you to travel on all manner and form of Berlin transport, including a trip to Posdam and the 109 bus back to Tegel airport when you leave.
- For cheap but filling snacks, try curry sausage, bockwurst or döner kebab in the *Schnellimbiss* fast food stalls.

Schnellimbiss: fast filling food

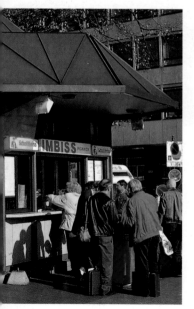

- Entry to museums is often free Sundays and national holidays.
- At cheaper hotels, check whether prices include breakfast, which, if it is a sturdy one, can save the cost of a big lunch.
- For a long stay, try the Mitwohnzentrale (see page 100), which arranges apartment accommodation.

SPECIAL EVENTS

February
Berlin International Film Festival Ten days of non-stop films in venues all over the city.

April
Free Berlin Art Exhibition The city's artists display their work at the exhibition centre in the Funkturm.

May
Berlin Drama Festival Performances throughout the city's theatres.

June
The **Berlin Philharmonic Orchestra** proclaims the beginning of summer and the end of its own season with a grand open-air concert at the Waldbühne in Charlottenburg.

July
The first two weeks of July see **Bach Days,** a festival of Baroque music, and a celebration of world music at the Haus der Kulturen der Welt.

September
Berlin Festwochen
Although all the arts are represented in this city-wide

Olympic Stadium, Charlottenburg

jamboree, music has a special place and the Philharmonie in Tiergarten is the star venue.

October/November
Jazz Fest Berlin All kinds of jazz, concentrated in the Tiergarten, at the Haus der Kulturen der Welt, the Philharmonie and Musikinstrumenten Museum.

December
The **Weinachtsmarkt** (Christmas market) appears on Breitscheidplatz and adjacent streets from 1 December to Christmas Eve.

SPORT

Berlin is not a particularly sporty city. Football is the most popular sport although local teams rarely make it into the first division. The German Football Association Cup Finals, Deutsche Pokalendspiele, are held in May/June in the Olympic Stadium in Charlottenburg. American football, also played at the Olympic Stadium, is becoming increasingly popular. The International Women's Tennis Championships are held in Berlin during one week in May. This is a rather up-market event reflecting the scarcity of

SPORT

playing facilities and their relatively high cost. The Berlin Marathon – the third largest after New York and London and enthusiastically supported by Berliners – takes place on the last Sunday in September. The race goes past all the major sights to end at Kaiser Wilhelm Gedächtniskirche in Breitscheidplatz. The half marathon is held on the first Sunday in April.

Not surprisingly, for a city so rich in rivers, lakes and canals, all kinds of watersports are available. Canoes can be hired by the hour, day, weekend or week from Kanu Connection, Köpenicker Strasse 9, Kreuzberg (tel: 612 2686). There is sailing and surfing on Wannsee and Mügelsee. Winter activities include skiing and skating. For a variety of sports under one roof, the enormous Sport und Erholungszentrum at Landsberger Allee, Friedrichshain (tel: 42 28 33 20) provides a comprehensive range of activities. Landessportbund Berlin, at Jesse-Owens-Allee 2, Charlottenburg Berlin 14053 (tel: 30 0020) publishes information about all sporting events and sporting facilities in Berlin in their *Freizeitsport-Kalender*.

Boaters navigate the backwaters of the Tiergarten's woods

DIRECTORY

Arriving

By air

British Airways have regular scheduled and charter flights direct to Tegel from Britain. Leading city-break operator Travelscene (Travelscene House, 11–15 St Ann's Road, Harrow, Middlesex HA1 1AS, tel: 0181 427 8800) offers good value all-in trips to Berlin. Schönefeld airport in the former East still mainly serves passengers entering from eastern European countries, Russia and so on. A frequent bus and taxi service from Tegel takes you to the main city terminus at Bahnhof Zoologischer Garten (Zoo station) and there are coaches from Schönefeld to the west. Tegel is not in the luxury class of airports but it has all the usual facilities – exchange, duty free shops and a good phone-link hotel booking system.

By land

Those travelling to Berlin by car have free access. If you qualify for a discount as a young person or senior citizen, travelling by train or coach may appeal; but check extra costs and journey time against air travel. Germany offers flat-rate rail tickets for unlimited travel within a specified time, and these may be available from other European countries, for all age groups.

Entry formalities

A valid passport is required by EU nationals and those of Australia, Canada, New Zealand and the US. Nationals of other countries must have a visa.

Camping

Berlin has four camping sites for tents and campers. They are all clean, well run and cheap but not central. Contact the German National Tourist Office in your country, or get in touch with the Deutschen Camping-Clubs eV Geisbergstrasse 11, Berlin 10777 (tel: 218 6071).

Chemist See **Pharmacies**

DIRECTORY

Crime

Berlin does not have a high crime rate, but take the usual precautions. Leave valuables and excess cash in hotel safes; do not flaunt large amounts of cash; carry money and other valuables in a secure pocket or money belt in crowded places such as markets.

Customs Regulations

Visitors from non-EU countries can take in 200 cigarettes or 25 cigars or 250 grams of tobacco, a litre of spirits and two litres of wine without paying duty. Visitors from EU countries can take in 300 cigarettes, or 75 cigars or 400 grams of tobacco, 1.5 litres of spirits and 5 litres of wine. There are no currency restrictions.

Disabled Travellers

For practical help and information about facilities for the disabled contact the Berliner Behindertenverband (Berlin Centre for the Disabled) Märkisches Ufer 28, Mitte, Berlin 10179 (tel: 274 1446).

Driving

You must have a valid driving licence. Drive on the right, pass on the left. Berliners complain about the growing density of their traffic but it is not a problem for most visitors from other cities. The speed limit on motorways is 130kmph (81mph); outside built-up areas 100kmph (62mph); and in built-up areas, 50kmph (31mph).

Pleasure boats on the Wannsee

Traffic regulations are strictly enforced, particularly in relation to speeding and use of alcohol. Fines are payable on the spot and the police may remove your car keys. At the time of German reunification the blood alcohol limit in East Germany was zero. Whatever the current situation you are advised to use public transport rather than drinking and driving.

Car Rental is *Autovermietung*. You must be over 21 and have driven for at least a year. International companies are represented at Tegel airport and major hotels.

Electricity
220 volts on a two-pin plug.

Embassies and Consulates
Australia Godesberger Allee 105–7, 5300 Bonn 2 (tel: (228) 81030).
Canada Friedrichstrasse 95, Berlin 10117 (tel: 261 1161).
United Kingdom Unter den Linden 32–4, Berlin 10117 (tel: 220 2431).
US Clayallee 170, Berlin 14169 (tel: 832 4087).

Emergency Telephone Numbers
Police 110
Fire 112
Ambulance 112
Medical assistance 31 00 31

Entertainment Information
Berlin-Program is published monthly by the tourist office, listing all major events of interest to the visitor. *Tip* and *Zitty* are two listings magazines which cover absolutely everything in all parts of the city.

They come out in alternate weeks and are available in all newsagents and kiosks.
The monthly English language magazine *Metropolis* carries feature articles as well as listings.

Health
No vaccinations are needed to enter Berlin. Citizens of other EU countries are entitled to free medical treatment, on production of Form E111. You must obtain this before leaving home, from your local main post office. It is always wise to take out travel insurance as well, in case of accident or illness.

Holidays
New Year's Day: 1 January
Good Friday, Easter Monday and Ascension Day; variable dates
Labour Day: 1 May
Day of Unity: 3 October
Day of Prayer and Repentance: third Wednesday in November
Christmas: 24 December (pm), 25 and 26 December

Lost Property
The main police lost property office (Fundbüro der Polizei) is the first port of call: Platz der Luftbrücke 6 (tel: 6990). If your property is stolen, report the incident to the nearest police station. You will need to complete a form which can then be used for any insurance claims. In the event of problems with language, translators are available, at no cost.
If your loss occurred on public transport, contact the BVG Lorenzweg 5, Tempelhof, Berlin 10773 (tel: 751 8021).

Media

Berliners have a huge appetite
for news. Their position at the
centre of conflict for so many
years has made them media
literate – a condition likely to
endure as the government
moves from Bonn to Berlin
accompanied by an attendant
army of journalists.
Foreign newspapers and
magazines are widely available
in the kiosks around Zoo Station,
Ku'damm and Europa-Center.
Of the German press, the most
substantial national dailies are
Die Welt and *Frankfurter
Allgemeine*. *Bild* is downmarket.
Local newspapers include *BZ*
(*Bild Zeitung*), *Tageszeitung*
(*Taz*), *Der Tagesspiel*, *Berliner
Morgenpost* and *Berliner
Zeitung*. Cable television is big
in Berlin, much of it
downmarket. For evening news
programmes, the BI channel
broadcasts a local news
programme, Abendschau, at
19.25hrs, followed by the
national news at 20.00hrs. Most
local radio stations play only
popular music. Berliner
Rundfunk on 19.4 is an
exception. BBC World Service
transmits on 90.2.

Money Matters

There are 100 Pfennigs (Pf) in
1 Deutsche Mark (DM). Coins: 1,
2, 5, 10, 20, 50 Pf and DM 1, 2, 5.
Notes: DM 10, 20, 50, 100, 500,
1000.
All banks are open Monday to
Friday 09.00–12.00hrs, and most
of them reopen on two weekday
afternoons (usually Tuesday and
Thursday), 14.00–18.00hrs, but
these times vary. The
Wechselstuben or money

exchanges in Zoo Station,
Europa-Center and
Friedrichstrasse Station have
longer opening hours.
Exchange rates are generally
more favourable at the
Wechselstuben.
Eurocheques are welcomed,
but credit cards are not much
used except in good hotels and
top restaurants. You can get a
cash advance on credit cards at
most major banks and the
money exchange at Zoo and
Friedrichstrasse Stations and
Europa-Center. In theory you
can make the same transactions
all over the city, but facilities are
still limited in the East.

Opening Times

Shops are open from Monday to
Friday 09.00–18.00hrs, and
Saturday mornings
09.00–13.00hrs. Larger stores
usually stay open late on one
evening of the week (Thursday)
and on the first Saturday of the
month. Museum opening times
vary although most are closed
on Mondays. They remain open
on all official holidays, and close
the day after.
The traditional practice of cafés
and bars closing one day a
week is always a surprise to
visitors, but this is also
changing.

Personal Safety

Berlin has always been known
for the safety of its streets and
public places. Things are
changing in this respect with
growing numbers of racist
incidents (particularly in the
East), but Berlin remains one of
the least threatening major cities
in Europe.

Pharmacies

A pharmacy is called an *Apotheke* and keeps normal shop hours. This is a place to buy drugs and medicines. If you are looking for general toiletries, you will find them cheaper in shops called *drogerien* or in department stores. A list of pharmacies open outside shop hours should be displayed on the Apotheke door. There is an emergency 24-hour pharmaceutical service (tel: 0 11 41).

Places of Worship

In this largely secular city, there are nevertheless many (Christian) Catholic and Protestant churches as well as mosques, temples and synagogues. A list of all places of worship is available from the Verkehrsamt, Tourist Office. For services in English, The American Church in Berlin

Berliner Dom's elegant cupola above the trees of Museumsinsel

maintains an ecumenical line at the Alte Dorfkirche, Onkel-Tom-Strasse 93 in Zehlendorf. The International Baptist Church holds services in English at Rothenburgstrasse 13, Steglitz. Evensong on Thursdays is conducted partly in English at the Berliner Dom, Lustgarten.

Police

Generally pleasant and helpful to tourists, Berlin *Polizei* – police – wear dark green uniforms. Violent protesters may get more than a taste of their own medicine. For emergency assistance, telephone 110.

Post Office

Post office is *Postamt*. The Zoo Station central post office is open from 06.00hrs to midnight Monday to Saturday; 08.00hrs to midnight on Sunday. Branch post offices are open from Monday to Friday 08.00–18.00hrs, and Saturday mornings until noon.

Post boxes are bright yellow. Letters for destinations outside Berlin should be posted through the slot marked 'Andere Richtungen' (other destinations).

Public Transport

A combination of buses, underground trains (U-Bahn), suburban surface trains (S-Bahn), and some ferry boats provide Berlin with an efficient public transport system. It is administered by the Berliner Verkehrs-Betriebe, or BVG, which has an information kiosk

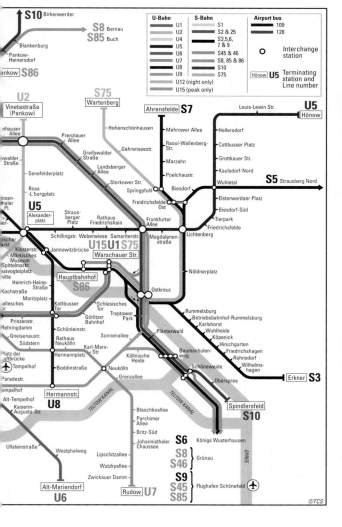

at Zoo Station. Services run from about 04.00hrs until around midnight (later on Saturday night). Night buses run a limited service. Tickets transferable between BVG bus, train and ferry services. Single fares are expensive – it makes more sense to buy a 24-hour (or weekly) Berlin ticket, which gives unlimited travel on buses and trains. Children under six travel free; children from six to 14 travel at reduced rates. Taxis are good value and are found at all termini and outside hotels, or can be hailed in the street. A tram system operates in the eastern part of the city. There are also pleasure boat cruises on city waterways (not BVG).

Senior Citizens
Production of an identity card will secure many reductions in entrance fees, river boat tickets and the like. A rich cultural life and relatively low crime rate make this an appealing city for older travellers.

Student and Youth Travel
Youth hostels are mostly single-sex dormitories and have a midnight curfew. Nonetheless you should book well ahead to be sure of a bed. If you are not already a member of the Youth Hostels Association, you can join at Jugend Zentrale, Tempelhofer Ufer 32, Kreuzberg, Berlin 10963 (tel: 264 9520). Bring passport and photo.

Telephones
Most phones are card operated in Berlin. Cards can be bought at the post office for DM12 or DM50. Cafés and bars often have coin operated public phones. There are metered pay phones and fax machines at the post office in Zoo Station.

Useful Numbers
National Directory Enquiries: 1188
International Directory Enquiries: 00118
Operator: 03
International Operator: 0010
Area code for West Berlin: (0) 30
To call West Berlin from Australia, dial 001; Canada or the US 011; New Zealand 00; the UK 00, followed by 49 30, followed by the number.
Codes from West Berlin are: Australia and New Zealand 00 61; Canada and US 001; UK 00 44.

Time
Berlin is one hour ahead of Greenwich Mean Time in winter and two hours ahead in summer.

Tipping
A service charge – Bedienung – is usually included in hotel and restaurant bills, but most people leave a little extra cash on top. It is usual to tip porters, maids, taxi drivers and washroom attendants.

Toilets
Public toilets usually carry the symbol of a man or woman or are labelled Herren (men); or Damen or Frauen (women). Most are free. Some are operated by a 10-Pf coin.

Tourist Offices
The main tourist office in former West Berlin – Verkehrsamt

Haus der Kulturen der Welt (fomerly Kongresshalle), given by the US

Berlin – is in the Europa-Center, Budapesterstrasse entrance. It is open daily 08.00–23.00hrs (tel: 262 6031/21234). The office in Zoo Station is also open during the same hours (tel: 313 9063). Another source of valuable information about the city, used by young people in particular, is the Informationszentrum at Hardenbergstrasse: open Monday to Friday 08.00–19.00hrs, and Saturday 08.00–16.00hrs. It provides useful publications in English which are not available at the Verkehrsamt. In the same building, the British Centre and, next door, the Amerika Haus are both good sources of information (and solidarity, if needed) for English-speaking visitors.

In the East, the major tourist office is in the Reisebüro at Alexanderplatz 5: open: Monday to Friday 08.00–20.00hrs, and weekends 09.00–18.00hrs. You can also change money here and reserve tickets for shows or trips. The Informationszentrum – tourist information office – beneath the Fernsehturm (TV Tower) (tel: 212 4675) will give you information on what to see in the city.

Overseas

Germany has tourist offices at:
Australia: Lufthansa House, 12th Floor, 143 Macquarie Street, Sydney 2000 (tel: (02) 367 3890).
Canada: 175 Bloor Street East, North Tower, 604, Toronto, M4W 3R8 (tel: (416) 968 1570).
UK: 65 Curzon Street, London W1Y 8NE (tel: (0171) 493 0080).
US: 122 East 42nd Street, Chanin Building, 52nd Floor, New York, NY10168–0072 (tel: (212) 661 7200).

LANGUAGE

Many Berliners can speak some English and many may be fluent; but efforts to speak German will be appreciated.

German has some special features. The letter ß is the same as 'ss'. There are capital letters at the start of all nouns; and 'the' may be *der*, *die* or *das* depending on whether a noun is masculine, feminine or neuter. If in doubt use *der*.

There are two ways to say 'you': always use the polite 'Sie' unless told otherwise. 'Du' is informal.

Basic Words and Phrases

yes ja
no nein
please bitte
thanks danke
good morning/day
guten Morgen/Tag
goodbye auf Wiedersehen
excuse me
entschuldigen Sie bitte
how are you?
wie geht es Ihnen?
very well, thanks; and you?
danke, gut; und Ihnen?

Rothes Rathaus, the city hall and seat of Berlin's mayor

do you speak English?
sprechen Sie Englisch?
I don't understand
Ich verstehe nicht
My name is...Ich heisse...

Where? wo?
when? wann?
today heute
tomorrow morgen
yesterday gestern
in the morning am Vormittag
in the afternoon am Nachmittag
in the evening am Abend

where is...? wo ist...?
bank? Bank?
station? Bahnhof?
airport? Flughafen?
bus-stop? Bushaltestelle?
police station? Polizeirevier?
toilets? Toiletten?
to the left nach links
to the right nach rechts
straight ahead geradeaus

open offen
closed geschlossen
good gut
bad schlecht
big gross
small klein
expensive teuer
cheap billig
how much does it cost?
wieviel kostet es?
(the) room (das) Zimmer
with bath mit Bad
Waiter! Herr Ober!
(the) menu (die) Speisekarte
breakfast Frühstück
lunch Mittagessen
dinner Abendessen
bread Brot
butter Butter
egg Ei

cheese Käse
vegetables Gemüse
fruit Obst
coffee Kaffee
tea Tee
beer Bier
wine Wien

**Monday, Tuesday,
Wednesday, Thursday, Friday,
Saturday, Sunday**
Montag, Dienstag, Mittwoch,
Donnerstag, Freitag,
Sonnabend, Sonntag

1 eins
2 zwei
3 drei
4 vier
5 fünf
6 sechs
7 sieben
8 acht
9 neun
10 zehn
11 elf
12 zwölf
13 dreizehn
14 vierzehn
15 fünfzehn
16 sechzehn
17 siebzehn
18 achtzehn
19 neunzehn
20 zwanzig
21 ein-und-zwanzig
30 dreissig
40 vierzig
50 fünfzig
60 sechzig
70 siebzig
80 achtzig
90 neunzig
100 hundert
500 fünfhundert
1,000 tausend

INDEX

INDEX/ACKNOWLEDGEMENTS

The Automobile Association wishes to thank the following photographers and
libraries for their assistance in the preparation of this book.

J ALLAN CASH PHOTOLIBRARY 82/3 Schloss Sanssouci, 84 Chinese
Teahouse Sanssouci.

MARY EVANS PICTURE LIBRARY 14/5 French Immigration to Berlin, 18
Cavalry attack, 20 Max Reinhardt.

NATURE PHOTOGRAPHERS LTD 88 White tailed eagle (E A Janes), 89
Common Crane (M E Gore), 90 Long-leaved sundew (P J Newman).

SPECTRUM COLOUR LIBRARY 78 Cecilienhof.

All remaining pictures are held in the Association's own library (AA PHOTO
LIBRARY) and were taken by ADRIAN BAKER with the exception of pages 35,
39, 57 which were taken by CLIVE SAWYER, pages 4, 33, 47, 49, 54, 63, 93,
99, 100, 105 and cover were taken by A SOUTER and pages 40/1 was taken
by D TRAVERSO.

Contributors:
For original edition: Copy editor Antonia Hebbert
For this revision: Copy editor Audrey Horne
Thanks to Gabrielle Macphedran and Adam Hopkins for their revisions